CUT
YOUR
BILLS

HAMLYN HELP YOURSELF GUIDE

CUT YOUR BILLS

MARGARET JONES

HAMLYN

First published in 1990 by
The Hamlyn Publishing Group Limited,
a division of the Octopus Publishing Group,
Michelin House, 81 Fulham Road,
London SW3 6RB

ISBN 0 600 57070 3

Typeset by Dorchester Typesetting Group Ltd

Printed and bound in Great Britain by
Collins, Glasgow

Contents

Introduction

Those little brown envelopes always seem to land on the door-mat at the worst times. The bills are bigger than you expect. Your first instinct is to panic, your next to assume that 'they' must have made a mistake.

You ring up the repairman and demand a breakdown of the costs. If it's a gas, electricity or phone bill you consider having the meter checked.

It's a common enough situation, especially in those purse-empty days after Christmas or when everything – mortgage, water, electricity, gas – seems to go up at the same time. Often it's the unexpected bill that throws your finances haywire.

At best it means you've got to start economising. At worst you may have to re-think all aspects of your spending.

This book shows you how to manage your money and to make savings in many different ways so that you don't land up in a desperate situation. And if the going gets tough it shows you how to cope.

Note: All prices, fares and other charges quoted in this book are current at the time of writing and subject to change.

ONE

Getting Organised

Mr. Micawber knew the situation well.

"Annual income twenty pounds, annual expenditure nineteen nineteen six, result happiness. Annual income twenty pounds, annual expenditure twenty pounds, ought and six, result misery."

Times may have changed but keeping tabs on spending so you don't go into the red is as much of a problem today as in Dickens's time.

It's often the unexpected bill – when the boiler breaks down in the middle of winter or the washing machine has to be replaced – that causes the biggest headache.

It may be the last straw when you are already struggling to meet ever-rising regular bills for electricity, gas, water and telephone – and a sky-high mortgage. Just paying your way becomes a daily battle. The good news is that it's a battle that can be won.

First you need to see how much money is coming in and where it is going. You probably have a general idea but you should know exactly. Once you've worked this out you can start to see where economies can be made and how a change in spending habits can pay off.

Some of the biggest bills can be cut significantly while others can be trimmed – without too much of a sacrifice.

Start A Filing System

This is the key to getting organised.

You'll need: three or possibly four box-type filing cases, some files to go in them, clip-on label holders and a strip of labels. A cardboard concertina-type filing case is cheaper and will do as well provided it's going to be strong enough to hold all the papers you'll be putting in it.

TIP *Check the small ads in your local papers to see if anyone is selling off second-hand filing boxes or even a filing cabinet.*

Everyone's circumstances are different but you might need files for: bank, car, community charge, credit cards, electricity, gas, holidays, home maintenance, insurance, loans (HP payments, overdrafts etc), mortgage, pension, salary, savings and investments, store accounts, tax, telephone, TV and/or video rental, water rates. You may also need files for: garden, maintenance payments, pets, private health insurance, school fees, subscriptions (clubs, magazines, trade unions etc).

It's worth having a file for guarantees and receipts. They are not part of your spending or outgoings but they can save you a lot of hassle and possibly money too if you buy something that goes wrong. If the name of the trader or the date of purchase isn't clear write it in before you file it.

It's useful to have a 'miscellaneous' file in which you can put odd items such as the TV licence, National Health Service and National Insurance numbers.

Once your filing system is set up put all bills and any letters referring to them into their files as soon as you've dealt with them.

You can also keep useful names, addresses and telephone numbers, including emergency numbers, in their appropriate file together with numbers of any accounts and credit cards.

TIP *While you're getting organised, make a note of the serial numbers of valuables such as the TV, video and hi-fi, the chassis numbers of your car and your car key . . . just in case. And file them safely.*

Check every item on a bill or bank or credit statement before you pay and file it away. This may seem obvious but when there are lots of demands on your time it's all too easy to look at the total sum and if it doesn't seem too outrageous assume it's all right and pay up.

Mistakes can happen or you might even be the victim of fraud. You could be accidentally charged twice for the same thing or be paying for goods and services you haven't had.

TIP *Never sign a credit card slip if the amount doesn't appear in the Total column. Unscrupulous traders have been known to add on other items and put in a bigger total. If you don't check the items on your account against your counterfoil you won't know if you've been swindled.*

If your bank statement is sent every three or six months ask for a monthly statement. It doesn't cost anything and will make it easier to keep control of your spending.

Everyday Spending

You're on your way now to getting your major bills organised. While they are the items that give you the shocks and may even put you in the red, they are only part of the picture. Everyday spending on things like food, cleaning materials, clothes, toiletries, and fares, also takes a major slice out of your income.

It helps to think of them as bills too – the food bill, the clothes bill etc. – because you can't see where the money goes and try to balance your budget without taking everything into consideration. Small items such as stamps, newspapers and bus fares can all add up to a substantial sum at the end of the week.

How can you keep track of this day-to-day spending? The best way is to write it all down. Buy a notebook, carry it with you and note down every item you spend money on – everything from a pot of tea and a cake in a cafe to a loaf of bread. Don't leave anything out. And don't forget to include things you pay for by cheque or credit card.

If you can do this for a month or six weeks you'll be able to see where money is being frittered, where you paid over the odds and where economies can be made. It requires a lot of self discipline but it will pay off in the end.

Use a notebook small enough to carry around with you, preferably one that can hold a pencil. A bright colour will be easy to find in a handbag.

Choose a time of year for your diary keeping when expenditure is fairly normal – not at Christmas or over a holiday period.

Taking Control

With the bills going into their files and your invaluable spending diary you can see exactly where the money is going. To check the overall position draw up a simple balance sheet. Get a large piece of paper and draw a line down the middle. Head one column INCOME and the other EXPENSES.

Under INCOME write down all the money you get during a month including all earnings, whether from a full-time job or part-time work, any pensions, building society income or investments or state allowances. Are you sure you are claiming all the allowances you are entitled to?

TIP *The Department of Social Security produce a booklet (FB2) called Which Benefit? that lists social security and NHS benefits that can be claimed. It's available from local DSS offices or the Citizens Advice Bureau.*

Under EXPENSES put down everyday spending for one month. If you've kept the diary for six weeks, the simple way to get your monthly total is to add it all up, divide by six and multiply by four – not too difficult with a calculator.

From the bills in your files work out how much each bill is costing you per month. Add up a year's bills and divide by twelve. Add this to your monthly average for everyday spending.

Finally add on a sum to cover occasional but heavy expenses for things like repairs to car or household appliances, new furniture or appliances, holidays, Christmas, new school uniforms for the children or a new winter coat for yourself.

Total it up and see how this figure compares with your total monthly income. You can now see whether you are managing your budget well or whether you are overspending. Don't forget that inflation will push up next year's bills and that you need savings available for emergencies.

Action Plan

You know how much you've got to trim your spending. The question now is where to make the cuts.

Start by making a breakdown of items in your everyday spending diary. Work out separate totals for your average monthly spending on food and drink, fares, toiletries and cosmetics, petrol, clothes, meals out, outings to the pub, cinema, theatre, club, sports centre etc. Just by going through these totals you should get some idea of where you can cut down.

For instance:

- Are you spending too much on outings? Having tea and cakes in a cafe may be a treat but are there times when you could take a flask of tea or coffee and have a picnic instead? When you take the children out they'll probably enjoy it more.

- Do you buy foods out of season when they're more expensive rather than waiting until they are cheaper? Fresh strawberries may make a change in the middle of winter but you can pay inflated prices for them. Although most fruit and veg are available all the year round there is a lot of pleasure in eating them in their season. They taste better too.

- Do you regularly have to throw away fruit or veg because you always buy too much?

- Do you fritter money on small purchases that take your eye such as gimmicky kitchen gadgets you'll never use?

One of the best ways to keep everyday spending under control is to get into the habit of making a shopping list and to stick to it. Manufacturers and retailers spend fortunes thinking up ways of getting you to buy their products.

The questions you have to ask yourself are: Do I really need this? Will I use it? Is it a bargain?

If the answer isn't 'yes' to all three, walk away and have a good think before committing yourself.

TIP *Carrying less money on you and leaving your chequebook and credit cards at home when you go shopping will make it easier to resist buying non-essentials.*

You probably won't need to study your big bills to know which ones make the biggest hole in your bank balance. We'll be looking at each of these in more detail further on. But as part of your economy plan ask yourself:

- Do all the regular bills arrive at the same time? If so you could ask if the payment dates can be altered to spread the load.

- Would it help if you could pay so much a month into a bank or building society account to help spread the cost?

- Could you reduce repair bills by DIY? Are there any local evening classes in car maintenance, plumbing, decorating or whatever you think you could do best?

- When there's a big service or repair job to be done on your home or car do you shop around? Cheapest isn't always best but it's worth asking around among friends and neighbours to see if there is someone they would recommend. You may be able to see examples of work they've already done.

- Do you buy too many things on credit? Unless it is interest-free, the total you'll pay will be much higher than if you'd saved up or taken the money from savings and paid cash.

- Have you too many credit and store card accounts? If you tend to get carried away because you can buy now and not worry about the bills until later consider reducing the number.

TIP *Do you always pay full price for everything? Look for cheaper outlets – so long as you don't have to sacrifice quality – and don't be afraid to ask if you can have a discount for paying cash.*

Where you put your money is as important as how you spend it. Is it working for you? Too much money sitting in a bank current account where it doesn't earn interest, is a waste. But don't let the account run down so low that you're in danger of being overdrawn.

Look for bank or building society accounts that will pay interest on your money.

Use your credit card to your advantage by paying off what you owe each month so you don't run up interest charges. If you have to pay an annual fee it may not be worth having. Take up perks that go with owning a credit card.

Shop around to ensure that any savings you have are in the best account for you. Make sure that some can be got at quickly in an emergency and put the rest into accounts or investments that have a longer notice period and pay higher interest.

If You Can't Pay

Sometimes, no matter how carefully you budget, a bill comes

along that you just can't meet. It's often the result of an emer-

gency such as the need for major repairs to house or car. Or it might be because high mortgage interest rates are gobbling up all your funds and leaving nothing for other expenses.

It's a nail-biting situation and you may feel like pushing the bills and reminders to one side in the hope that a solution will come along. In your heart you know this is unlikely and it will only make the situation worse if you delay.

Don't panic and don't waste time. The sooner you tell people that you can't pay their bill the easier it is going to be to sort out the problem. Explain your difficulties and be ready to offer some payment towards the bill.

At this stage it is usually possible to work out a way in which the bill can be paid off, maybe in small amounts over a long period.

Avoid borrowing your way out of trouble if you possibly can. Taking out one loan to pay off all the others may seem the best solution. But if you can't keep up repayments on that one you could be in even bigger trouble.

Priorities

The consequences of not paying can be more serious with some bills than with others.

If there are several bills you can't pay put them in order of priority. If you don't keep up payments on the mortgage or rent you could lose your home. If you don't pay electricity, gas, water or telephone bills you can be cut off. If you don't pay the community charge or tax bills your possessions could be seized by bailiffs.

So if you are having trouble paying any of these bills, act quickly. However difficult your circumstances they will try to work out something with you. With less vital bills you may be able to persuade your creditors to give you time.

If you can't cope, contact your local Citizens' Advice Bureau or money advice centre, if there is one. They will help you sort out your problems.

TWO

Fuel

Fuel bills are among the biggest but they are also the ones where you can make big savings.

You can't do much about the size of your mortgage but there are few homes where the cost of heating, hot water and power can't be cut. There are two ways to do this:

- By simple inexpensive economies.

- By ensuring that your home is well insulated and that you have an efficient heating system.

Simple Economies

Depending on how draughty your home is, draught-proofing can save up to 10% on your fuel bill. You'll not only be more comfortable but you'll get back what you spend within a year or two in savings on fuel bills.

If you can afford to pay the extra, it's better to buy the more long-lasting materials for the job. But if it's a question of keeping out draughts for now as cheaply as possible there's a good choice here too. Your local DIY or hardware store should be able to help.

Start by draught-proofing windows and outside doors. Adhesive foam strip is cheap and easy to fit. Metal and plastic strip, although dearer and a little harder to fit, will last longer.

If the wind whistles through your letter-box fit a cover on the inside. These are usually flaps or brush-type seals that prevent draughts even when there is something stuck into the box. Fit a decorative keyhole cover.

As a cheap form of double glazing cover the inside window frames with clingfilm. It may only last one winter and you won't be able to open the windows but you can do the whole house for £3-£4.

Wall-to-wall carpeting, ideally with good felt or rubber underlay, helps to reduce heat loss through the floor. If you don't have a fitted carpet, seal large gaps between the floor and skirting boards with foam strip attached to beading or plastic wood or with newspaper.

TIP *Newspapers spread under rugs or carpets will keep out draughts and give added warmth.*

Fill up any ceiling cracks and seal gaps where pipes pass through ceilings or walls. If you have a chimney but no longer use the fire, block it up with a piece of chipboard but make a few holes in it first for ventilation.

It's important to allow air to circulate, especially if there is a fuel-burning appliance in the room. Open fires, gas fires, flued boilers and flueless appliances such as gas cookers and bottled-gas heaters or paraffin heaters need fresh air to burn their fuels safely and efficiently.

There should be a permanent supply of air into the room, possibly from an air brick. Appliances with a balanced flue draw the air directly from outside. Never block up air bricks or ventilating grilles.

Other cheap and easy ways to keep warmth in your home:

■ Put aluminium foil behind radiators on outside walls to deflect heat back into the room. Kitchen foil will do although there are proprietary brands which may be easier to put up.

■ Fit shelves above radiators to stop the heat going straight up to the ceiling and encourage it to circulate.

■ Put up thick lined curtains and draw them in all rooms as soon as it gets dusk. Ensure they are above or behind radiators.

■ Check that radiators are not blocked by furniture which stops the heat circulating.

■ Put sausage-shaped draught excluders at the bottom of doors. You can make one easily by stuffing a stocking with oddments of material.

- Get damaged radiants on gas fires replaced. They're the parts that throw out the heat.

Fact About 20p in every £ spent on energy goes on hot water.

The biggest saving you can make is to put a thick jacket round your hot water tank – it should be three inches thick. There are lots of cheap thin jackets in the shop but they won't keep in the heat very effectively. Look for one made to the specification British Standard 5615: 1985. The price will vary depending on size, expect to pay around £10 but you'll get that back in lower fuel bills within the year.

Putting a jacket on an uninsulated tank can cut your hot water bills in half. If the jacket already on your tank is thin or worn you'll save money by putting another on top.

If the cylinder needs replacing you can now buy one with a preformed foam insulation jacket. It's less bulky and will leave more room in the airing cupboard.

You can make more savings by:

- Turning down the thermostat on the hot water cylinder (if there is one) to 60 degrees C or 140 degrees F or less. This should provide enough hot water for an average family.

- Making sure that hot water pipes are well wrapped. Give priority to wrapping the hottest ones and those near cold places. You can buy split tubing made either of polyurethane foam or rubber, or rolls of felt strip. Make sure it's fire resistant.

- Turning down the hot water thermostat if your hot water is too hot to use without adding cold. That means it's set too high and wasting energy.

- Taking a shower instead of a bath – you can have five for the cost of one bath.

- Waiting until you have a full load before you use the washing machine. If you don't have enough for a full load use the economy or half load programme if your machine has one. Use a cool water wash programme if possible.

■ Stacking the washing up until you have a full load – if you can stand the sight of unwashed dishes.

■ Making sure taps are turned off properly and getting them repaired if they drip. In just one day a fast dripping hot tap could waste enough hot water to fill a bath.

■ Always using a bowl to wash dishes or hands in instead of doing it under a running tap. Rinse dishes under a cold tap.

Immersion Heater – On or Off? If you depend on an immersion heater and you're home all day and use a fair amount of hot water it's probably best to leave it on. But when there's no one home during the day or if you don't use a lot during the day switch it on for when you need it and off again once the hot water is running.

Fact About 30p in every £ spent on energy bills goes on cooking, lighting and electrical appliances.

You can reduce this bill by:

■ Remembering that a microwave oven, pressure cooker, multi cooker, mini oven, electric casserole/slow cooker, divided pan or steamer can all be cheaper than a conventional oven.

■ Cooking several dishes together in the oven.

■ Using the grill not the oven for small things like chops.

■ Making sure that the base of pans just cover the cooker ring; if you use gas adjust the flame to cover the pan base.

■ Putting lids on pans and turning down the heat as soon as liquid starts to boil.

■ Not heating more water than you need in the kettle, although there should be enough water to cover the element in an electric one. Regular descaling keeps it efficient so you're not using more electricity to heat water than you need. Rinse well afterwards or keep a descaler inside.

■ Cutting food small before putting it in the pan so that it cooks more quickly.

Try to ensure that your fridge or freezer is not near anything hot such as the oven or boiler. If you've no choice try to leave a gap between them. They'll use less electricity if they're regularly defrosted and kept at least three quarters filled.

If your freezer is too big for your needs fill it up with non-food things such as newspapers, towels and plastic containers filled with water. Load food in quickly and don't open the door any more than you need.

Let warm food cool down before you put it in the fridge or freezer. Warm food and warm air can lead to a build-up of extra frost which can make the fridge work less efficiently.

Check that the seal works well by closing the door on a thin strip of paper. It should be tightly gripped and not slide easily. Worn door seals can be replaced quite cheaply.

Try to have one big ironing session.

Lighting doesn't add a lot to your energy bill but if you regularly leave lights on unnecessarily the cost mounts up. But make sure that you don't leave dark areas which may be dangerous (such as stairs), especially for children or the elderly.

Fluorescent tubes and compact energy-saving bulbs use a quarter of the electricity usually required by ordinary filament bulbs for the same amount of light. And they can last five times as long. They cost more but you recoup this with the energy they save. If you are going to have a light on for three hours or more a day it would pay you to use fluorescent tubes or energy-saving bulbs. Switching fluorescent tubes on and off shortens their lives.

Directional lights are good for reading and other close work.

Bigger Savings

Fact About 35% of your energy bill pays for heating.

Sometimes you have to spend money in order to make a saving. Insulating the home can cost anything from a few hundred to several thousands £s, depending on the property and how far you want to go. Put in as much insulation as you can. You'll reduce your bills and enjoy greater comfort.

The Loft

Start at the top of the house by insulating the loft. Even if there is some insulation there already, topping it up should pay for itself in less than three years. If there is no insulation there at all you'll get your money back within two years.

The most effective materials are mineral fibre blanket, and blown mineral wool or celullose fibre which you can get at DIY or hardware stores or builders' or plumbers' merchants.

You'll need a thickness of at least 100mm (4ins) but preferably 150mm (6ins).

It's not too difficult to do yourself and you'll save money but it can be uncomfortable and you may prefer to pay an expert to do it for you.

Cracks and holes in the upstairs ceiling allow warm moist air to escape into the loft. This can cause condensation. So fill them up before you start. If you are using mineral wool which can irritate the skin and throat you'll need a dust mask, rubber gloves and clothing that covers you well.

Keep the hatch closed while you work and empty any left-over material into a bag while you're in the loft. When you've finished put the mask in the dustbin and wash all clothing including gloves.

Don't forget to insulate the hatch and to put draught strip round the edge. The loft will be colder once it's insulated so wrap up all pipes, the cold water tank and any other tanks. But don't put insulating material underneath them so they can get warmth from the house below to stop them freezing in winter.

TIP Grants for loft insulation and draught-proofing are available for some families and pensioners on low incomes. New renovation grants are designed to help the most hard-up who are living in houses in the worst conditions to help bring them up to acceptable standards. If you think you might qualify, see your local council's home improvements grants officer before you start work.

Cavity Walls

Fact Up to half the heat loss in an average house goes straight through the walls.

Cavity wall insulation can stop at least half this loss and should therefore make a significant reduction in the heating bill as well as making your house more comfortable.

The cost depends on the type of fillings used and the size of your house but it is much less than most people think. For a terrace house, for instance, it will cost around £300 with a foam fill and £400 for a polystyrene or wool fill. For a detached house the figures are £500+ or £600+. It cuts around £100 a year off the average heating bill and so has paid for itself after about four years.

Most houses built after 1930 have cavity walls which means that the external wall of the house consists of two walls with a small air gap in between. You can generally tell if your house has cavity walls by looking at the pattern of the brickwork. Most of the bricks will be nine inches long.

When you have cavity-wall insulation the gap between the two walls is filled with insulating material.

It's not a DIY job but one for an approved contractor. To find one in your area contact the National Cavity Insulation Association, which is the national trade association covering all processes. Their address is: PO Box 12, Haslemere, Surrey GU27 3AN. Tel. (0428) 54011.

Solid Wall Insulation

Houses with solid walls lose more heat than those with cavity walls. Proper insulation can stop up to two thirds of this loss.

You can either insulate the walls internally or externally.

Internally, wall insulation can be done by a DIY enthusiast for around £800 (£1,200 if you use a contractor). The work is done with plasterboard/insulation laminates made up of plasterboard with a backing of insulation and a built-in vapour check. They are called thermal boards and have to be ordered from builders' merchants.

Externally, wall insulation is a job for a specialist contractor. Find one in your area through the External Wall Association, PO Box 12, Haslemere, Surrey GU27 3AX. Tel: (0428) 54011.

The choice of surface finishes includes rendering, resin coating, cladding boards, tiles, slates and pebble dash.

TIP *The thicker the insulation the more you'll save on heating bills and you won't pay proportionately more for having extra thickness.*

Double Glazing

Fact Single-glazed windows lose up to 25% of your heat.

Double glazing can halve this loss. It insulates by creating a pocket of air trapped between two panes of glass. As it doesn't mix with the air in the room or the air outside it creates an insulating barrier.

How much you save depends on the number and size of windows, the house and how warm you want to keep it. It will cut out draughts and cold spots, reduce noise, help solve condensation problems and make your home feel cosier.

But compared with other forms of insulation, it's expensive for the amount of energy it saves. Professionally installed double glazing is rarely justified simply on money-saving grounds. It could be worthwhile though if a window frame or frames need replacing anyway.

It's considerably cheaper to fit it yourself. Most systems come in kit form ready for home assembly and installation. Sometimes a firm will make up secondary windows to your measurements, cutting the frames to size and fixing the glaze, leaving you to fit them.

TIP *If you use solid fuel or logs buy as much as you can in the summer when prices are lowest. Phone around to find the cheapest price first. If your neighbour uses the same fuel you may be able to get it cheaper by bulk buying together.*

You can order factory-made units from a glass or builders' merchant which are tailor-made to the size you want but your window frames must be in good condition to take the extra weight and your measurements must be precise. If you make the slightest error in your measurements you could be left with expensive frames that don't fit and can't be trimmed.

The cheapest and easiest DIY double glazing is plastic cling-film (mentioned earlier). Fixed panels of glass or rigid sheets of plastic make inexpensive secondary double glazing. Fix in place either with double-sided adhesive tape or magnetic strips. They should be easily removable in case of fire.

Professional Double Glazing

You should get quotations from three or four firms. Ask neighbours and friends who have had double glazing installed fairly recently if they would recommend the firm that did the job. There are a lot of cowboys in this business and personal recommendation by someone you know is a good indication that you are dealing with a reliable business. You can also see the quality of their work for yourself.

Check whether the firm is a member of the Glass and Glazing Federation (GGF) which has a code of practice endorsed by the Office of Fair Trading. It includes an advisory service and an arbitration scheme if you run into problems.

Some double-glazing salesmen go for the hard sell. They offer big discounts and other incentives if you agree to sign up with them there and then.

Recent legislation aimed at curbing cowboy traders now gives people who sign agreements at home a seven day cooling-off period in which they can change their minds. This doesn't apply though if you have invited a salesman to call. But you are covered anyway if you are dealing with a member of the GGF.

Heating Controls

The more control you have over your heating and hot water system the more you can save. To operate your central heating efficiently and economically you should have: a time clock or programmer, a central room thermostat and/or thermostatic radiator valves, a hot water tank thermostat and a motorised valve or valves.

You can set the controls to fit in with the times you want hot water or the heat to come on, and adjust them to a comfortable temperature.

■ The programmer sets the times you want the boiler to go on and off.

■ The room thermostat or thermostatic valves control the

23

temperature in your rooms so you're not wasting heat.

■ The hot water thermostat stops tap water getting too hot.

■ Motorised valves stop water flowing either to the hot water cylinder or to the radiators when they are not needed. So in summer you can have hot water without also heating up the central heating system.

Timers and programmers cost from around £30, and room thermostats, thermostatic valves and hot water thermostats all cost from around £10. They'll soon pay for themselves in savings on the fuel bill.

If you started with no controls and put these in you would knock 30p in the £ off your heating costs.

TIP *Heating bills can be cut by 8% just by turning the thermostat down by one degree. But don't overdo it if there are elderly people, invalids or young children in the house.*

The Boiler

The more efficient your boiler the more you will save on heating costs. A modern boiler uses less fuel than an older model to produce the same amount of heat.

If yours is more than ten years old you could cut heating bills by up to 10% by replacing it – especially if the old one is oversized for its job. If you've improved the insulation in your house you might be better off with a lower output boiler.

If your old boiler doesn't have proper controls on it and the new one does you could slash your heating bills by 25% or even more. You wouldn't save quite so much by replacing a solid fuel boiler.

A qualified central heating installer should be able to tell you whether it would be worth changing over. Ask friends if they can recommend someone. If you have difficulty finding an installer one of the trade associations may be able to help.

They include:

Confederation for the Registration of Gas Installers (CORGI), St Martin's House, 140 Tottenham Court Road, London W1P 9LN Tel 071 387 9185.

Heating and Ventilating Contractors' Association, 34 Palace Court, London W2 4JG Tel 071 229 2488. Home Heating Link Line (0345) 581158.

Institute of Plumbing, 64 Station Road, Hornchurch, Essex Tel (04024) 72791.

National Association of Plumbing, Heating and Mechanical Service Contractors, 6 Gate Street, London WC2A 3HP.

Get at least three quotations before you decide on a new system. Ask for one that is tailored to your needs, rather than a standard package.

TIP *Do you really need central heating? In a small well-insulated house it may be just as cost effective to have individual room heaters.*

Condensing boilers cost more than conventional boilers but are the most efficient available. Unlike an ordinary boiler their efficiency remains high even when working at a low level output such as in the summer. They are more suitable for a medium to large sized house where the extra installation costs can be more quickly offset by savings on gas bills.

Fact In the new city of Milton Keynes, home owners' fuel bills are 30% or more lower than in the rest of the country. That's the result of experiments with solar heating and the building of energy-efficient housing that can match Scandinavian homes.

The lessons learned are being offered to the rest of the country through a charity: The National Energy Foundation.

TIP *If you are on Economy 7 tariff make sure you know when you receive off-peak electricity and make the fullest use of it. If you have a timer you can set it to start your washing machine during the cheap rate hours.*

Paying the Bill

If you have trouble meeting large winter fuel bills there are various schemes to help you spread the cost.

■ You can buy £1 energy stamps from gas showrooms, electricity shops and from some sub Post Offices. Gas and electricity stamps are interchangeable and can be used to pay both bills.

25

They are particularly popular with pensioners who buy them when they draw their pensions. The advantage is that they take the edge off the big bills. The drawback is that the money could otherwise be earning interest in a bank or building society account – or you could lose them.

■ Gas and electricity boards run their own budget payment schemes in which you pay the same amount each month. It is calculated by estimating the total of your bills for a year and dividing it into 12 equal payments. These are made by direct debit from your bank account each month. Adjustments for over or under payments apply at the end of the budget year.

Again it ties up money in advance and if the estimate is too high you'll be paying in more than you need. If it's an under-estimate you'll still end up with a bill to pay at the end of the year. But if you don't mind this it may be worthwhile for peace of mind.

TIP *Start payments in the autumn and you'll get what is, in effect, an interest-free loan during the winter months when you use most fuel.*

■ You can arrange to pay what you like when you like towards your next gas or electricity bill under easy payment schemes operating in some areas.

■ Banks, building societies and finance houses operate budget accounts for paying all household bills. You estimate the total for all your household bills over the coming year and pay one twelfth of the total into the account each month.

You then pay the bills from this account either by cheque or standing order. 'Save and Borrow' type accounts work the same way. Some of these accounts pay interest when you're in credit but you may have to pay a fee and the charge can be fairly high if you get overdrawn. See what your bank can offer.

■ A pre-payment meter enables you to pay for your electricity or gas as you use it. It is an expensive way of paying for fuel.

If you are a well-organised person, the best way to spread the cost is to set up your own budget account. Use an account with a bank or building society that pays interest on your money. Add up all the bills you expect in the coming year and add on something extra for inflation. Divide the total by twelve and put that amount into the account each month. Pay your major bills from this account.

Check Your Bill

If you get a bill that seems too high it may be because: there has been a price rise; it is an estimate; you have used more energy than you realized; you've recently bought a new appliance that uses more electricity; you've had someone ill at home or visitors; the weather was very cold; your meter is wrong.

The accounts office will tell you if there has been a price rise.

You can see whether it's an estimate because there will be a letter E beside the meter reading. If you consider the estimate to be too high check it against the bill for the same period last year. (Ensure that that wasn't also estimated and on the low side.)

Better still, read your meter and see if they have over-estimated the amount you've used. If they have, fill in the Estimated Reading box on the back of your bill and send it off promptly. You may be able to telephone the figure to the accounts office – see what it says on the back of the bill. You should then get a revised bill.

TIP *If there's a price rise due, it could pay you not to get an over-estimated bill revised. The extra will be knocked off your next (higher rate) bill. But if the bill has been under-estimated and you decide to leave it and pay the extra on the next one you could end up paying more if there's a price rise in the meantime.*

How To Read Your Meter

Electricity There are two kinds of meter. The digital meter shows a line of numbers like you see on a car mileometer. (Ignore the last figure on the right.) That's the total number of units used. Compare it with the total shown on your bill. Off-peak meters usually have two lines of numbers, one for units used during off-peak hours and the other for units used during the rest of the time. Compare these figures with those shown on your bill.

27

If your meter has dials start with the far left dial and write down the figures that the hands point to. If a hand is between numbers write down the lower figure. Ignore the very small dial which is usually red. The figures you have written down show you the number of units used.

Gas If there is a line of numbers they show the total amount of gas used. If there are dials write down the figures that the hands point to on the four bottom dials from left to right. Again, if the hand is between two figures write down the lower figure.

Don't wait until you've got a query to check your meter. If you read it at the beginning of each quarter and write down the reading and then read it again, perhaps weekly to begin with, you can check how much you are using. You can also see how much this is costing.

To check your electricity consumption add up the number of units used in a week and multiply it by the price per unit which is shown on your bill. (Don't forget there'll be a standing charge to pay on top of your quarterly bill.)

You can do the same with the gas bill. To make it easier the Gas Consumers' Council have produced a Gas Cost Guide which shows at a glance how much the gas you've used costs. It's available from regional offices. The address and telephone number is on the back of your gas bill.

If you can't otherwise account for an unexpectedly high bill and there hasn't been a clerical error along the line, you can ask to have the meter checked. This should be a last resort as you may end up paying for the test if there's nothing wrong with the meter. You don't pay anything if the meter is found to be faulty.

TIP *To check whether your meter is overcharging switch everything off except say a small heating appliance and see if the meter is whirling round. Switch off the appliance and see if the meter has stopped whirling. Allow a minute or so for it to run down. Make sure everything is switched off. One man who tried to test his meter this way was convinced it was wrong. Later he found he'd left a heater switched on in his attic all winter!*

Can't Pay?

Tell the gas or electricity company as soon as you realise that you can't pay the bill. Don't wait until they send you a final demand or, worse still, cut you off. The sooner they know you're in difficulty the easier it will be to come to some sort of arrangement to pay it off.

If you have great difficulty budgeting for fuel you may be better off with a pre-payment meter. It's a more expensive way of paying for gas and electricity but at least your supply won't be cut off.

Codes of Practice

The gas and electricity industries both have a code of practice for domestic customers which now forms part of their licenses. Under this you can't be cut off if:

- You agree to keep to a payment arrangement and pay off the debt by instalments within a reasonable period. The arrangement would take account of your circumstances and income. You can make an offer or the amount may be decided for you;

- It is safe and practical to install a slot meter. This would be set to collect the debt within a reasonable period and the amount would take account of your circumstances and income;

- The debt is in the name of a past customer and you have made proper arrangements for the gas or electricity companies to take over the supply;

- There is no adult at home at the time – unless you have been given warning that you are to be disconnected on or after a particular date;

- The debt is only for something you have bought on credit at a gas or electricity showroom.

Customers can't be cut off between October 1 and March 31 if all the people in the house are old age pensioners. This doesn't apply if they can pay but haven't.

THREE

Telephone

The simplest way to keep your telephone bills down is to:

- Make your calls in the cheap rate period as far as possible;

- Keep calls short;

- Avoid using premium rate services;

- Avoid using the operator if you can;

- Weigh up the advantages (or otherwise) of sending a letter instead.

It's only too easy to pick up the phone on impulse when you suddenly remember that you have to make a call. But if you do it during the peak rate period it can cost you a packet. A local call is five times dearer if you make it at noon during the week rather than waiting until the cheap rate starts at 6 pm.

The cheap rate period runs from 6 pm until 8 am from Monday to Friday, all day Saturday and Sunday and at Christmas and New Year.

The standard rate of charge applies from 8 am to 9 am and from 1 pm until 6 pm Monday to Friday.

The peak rate – the most expensive time to make a call – is from 9 am until 1 pm Monday to Friday.

TIP *If you call a business and the switchboard operator can't put you through because the person you want to speak to is already speaking on the phone don't hang on. Leave a message to say you will ring again or to ask the person you want to call you back. Your call is charged from the moment it is answered. So making a second call is cheaper than waiting to be put through.*

Every minute you spend on the phone is adding to your bill. Before you make a call think what you are going to say. Make notes of any questions you want to ask if it helps. Make your points quickly and end the call as soon as you reasonably can.

Don't be tempted to repeat what you've already said – a common and expensive habit – or to add unnecessary bits of information.

You can buy a device which shows the units you are using as you make the call. Or you can keep a timer by the phone and pre-set it to ring at the time when you should be ending the call. Be firm with friends who want to chatter on at your expense.

Cordless phones can tempt you to keep chattering, especially if you are in the habit of walking around the house as you talk.

If you are on a modern digital exchange you can ask for a call barring facility. It will add an extra £7 to your quarterly rental. There are two types, one which bars all calls other than 999 ones, and another which allows local calls but bars long distance ones.

So if you are going out for the evening and leaving a house full of teenagers behind you can restrict the calls they can make.

By 1995 the whole country will have been switched from the old electro-mechanical exchanges to digital ones and call barring will be one of many new high-tech services on offer.

Or you can buy a BT approved call barring panel for around £20 that fits over any BT wall socket. When you turn the key only outgoing 999 calls can be made. If you forget to bar calls before you leave the house, you will soon be able to call up your phone and instruct it by remote control to stop outgoing calls.

One of the advantages of digital exchanges is that customers get itemised bills for calls that cost 50p or more, although not all of the new high-tech exchanges have this service yet.

With the Mercury telephone system, not yet available in all areas, all calls are itemised on the bill.

TIP *If you want to have a phone in the bedroom at night or in some other part of the house but don't want to go to the cost of*

31

having a new socket put in, you can buy a DIY extension kit for around £10. It's like an extension lead: you plug one end into the nearest telephone point and the other into your telephone which you can then take into another room.

Ringing Up The Bills

Some calls cost extra and can bump up your bill dramatically. They include:

- Premium Rate Services. They offer information or entertainment and usually start with the number 0898, 0836 or 0077. They include about a dozen chat-lines as well as information about the weather, motoring conditions, cricket scores, recipes, children's bedtime stories and many other services. They cost 38p a minute at any time of the day and 25p a minute during the evening and weekends. Addicts have run up bills of thousands of £s.

- Transferred Charge Calls. They cost an extra 35p on top of the normal charge. It's better to make a quick call if you can and ask the person at the other end to ring you back.

- Any Calls made through the Operator. Even in the cheap rate period a local call via the operator costs 51p for three minutes, a long distance call 79p for three minutes.

- Advice of Duration and Charge (ADC). To find out how much a particular call has added to your bill costs 75p if it's for a local or national call, 98p for an international call.

- Personal Call. If you don't want to waste money hanging on while somebody goes to find the person at the other end, you can ask for a Personal Call. You are charged only when the person you want answers. The service costs £2.21.

- An Alarm Call. This can help wake you up in the morning if you don't trust your alarm clock. It costs £1.21.

- A Fixed Time Call. This is where you arrange for the operator to put a call through at a particular time and it costs £2.01.

- Calls to a Cellular phone. These phones are usually used in cars and calls cost from 38p per minute at peak periods to 25p at off-peak periods, regardless of distance. If anyone asks you to call them on a number that starts with either 0860 or 0836 – the cellular network codes – wait until you can call them on an ordinary phone, if possible.

TIP *Freefone numbers are just what they say. You can make the call and won't be charged.*

TIP *An answerphone that you can switch on to record calls when you are not at home or too busy to talk to anyone can be a boon. But you also have to return those calls! Switching on only when you are expecting a call you don't want to miss instead of switching it on automatically every time you leave the house means you don't have so many calls to return.*

Rent Or Buy

Undecided about whether to continue renting your phone from BT or to buy? You are probably going to be better off buying than renting. But consider what's important to you.

Renting

If you rent: You don't own the phone and will continue to pay a rental charge to BT for the line and the telephone. The more sophisticated the telephone the higher the rental.

If anything goes wrong with your phone they will repair or replace it free of charge.

If there's a fault on the line they will repair it free whether your telephone is rented or not.

Buying

If you buy: You own the phone and you won't pay rental for it to BT. But the biggest part of the quarterly rental is for the use of the exchange line and you will continue to pay this.

The telephone will be covered for the first year by the guarantee. After that you are responsible for paying for any repairs.

You may be able to take out a maintenance contract once the guarantee is up. If you buy your phone from BT the maintenance contract will cost £3 a quarter for a standard phone.

As you can buy a new phone for £25 or less you may well feel that it's not worth paying this extra just in case it breaks down.

If the phone won't work find out whether the trouble is in the phone or on the line – or you could end up paying BT's call-out charge even though the phone hasn't been repaired.

Tip *To find out whether the phone is faulty unplug it and try another phone in the same socket. If you haven't a second phone borrow one from a neighbour. If that one works you'll know that the phone is faulty. Take it back to the shop where you bought it. If the second phone doesn't work, the fault is almost certainly on the line. Call BT.*

What to Check If your phone was installed some years ago you may need a new-style master socket and maybe extension sockets. Contact BT for details.

If your phone is going to run off the BT network (not Mercury) any phone you buy must be BT approved. It will have a swing ticket showing a green circle. Second-hand phones sometimes sold from barrows or market stalls could be illegal non-approved ones.

Tip *If a fault develops on the line so you can't receive or make calls and BT fails to repair it within two working days of you reporting the fault, you can claim compensation. Unless they can prove that it was because of circumstances beyond their control, you're entitled to £5 a day for every day you were without the service after the two working days. You can also claim compensation if BT misses an appointment to install an exchange line and then fails to come within two working days of the appointment.*

When You Buy If you are thinking of buying a new phone, shop around: specialist telephone shops are not necessarily the cheapest. Prices can vary by as much as £40.

You can buy a cheap and cheerful phone for anything from £5 to £15 or one with more facilities for £70-£80. Transmission on the cheapest phones may not be as good as those that cost more. A medium-price phone should have what you basically need and give good quality reception. After that you are paying for extras.

TIP *Decide which features you want and don't pay extra for any you're not likely to use. Many of these features are of more use to people who spend a lot of time on the phone.*

Most people find it handy to have a button that will call up the last number dialled, especially when that number is constantly engaged.

It's also useful if the phone has a memory that can store the numbers you use most often. You programme them in. Then when you want to call up, say your mother, you press just one button and your phone calls her number.

If you fancy a cordless phone, weigh up whether you need one or whether it wouldn't be cheaper to have additional sockets fitted in your home to give you the extra flexibility without the expense. Cordless phones cost more – between £70 and £130 – because they use a two-way radio link that is more complicated.

· Some cordless phones don't have full back-up batteries and won't work if there's a power failure. Recently approved cordless phones have full battery back-up and will work for some hours after a power failure.

If you do buy a cordless phone, and it's the only one you have, check that the base unit, as well as the handset, includes battery back-up.

TIP *If you get a wrong number or crossed or noisy line or are cut off, call the operator, explain what has happened and ask for a reconnection. Ask to have the cost of the unsatisfactory call credited to your account.*

If your local exchange has been converted to a digital system or is likely to be in the next year or so look for a phone that can be switched from pulse dialling to tone dialling. This will enable you to use the facilities that the new high-tech exchanges will be offering. Ask your local BT office for more details.

TIP *When you ask to have the telephone service you are contracted to have it for at least a year. But if you leave the UK for two or three months, perhaps to spend the winter in sunny Spain, you can tell BT that you want the service suspended* *while you're away. You won't then have to pay rent for that peri-od. You will have to pay for the service to be restored but it still works out cheaper than the quarterly rental.*

When you find a phone you like, try it out in the shop to see if it is easy and comfortable to use. Try out the different fea-tures if you can, to see how they work.

TIP *Specially designed phones are available for handicapped people. They include such features as: handsets, special couplers that can be used with NHS hearing aids, flashing lights on the handset and enlarged buttons or dial numbers. Your local BT sales office should be able to give advice.*

Bills

Just like the gas and electricity industries. BT offers various budget schemes to help soften the blow when the bill arrives.

You can pay by direct debit from your bank account, or by monthly instalments through a budget account on a Standing Order with your bank, or you can buy Telephone Stamps from the Post Office or a BT shop.

If you find it hard to manage your budget, any of these schemes will give you peace of mind. But with all of them you are paying money up-front that could otherwise be earning you money in an interest-paying account.

As with gas and electricity bills, the ideal way to cope is to work out how much your bills are likely to total in a year, add on something for inflation, divide by twelve and pay this sum into a budget account with a bank or building society that pays interest.

When the bills come in, pay from this account.

TIP *People who make little use of their phone, such as pen-sioners who may have it mainly for in-coming calls, can get a 25% rebate off the rental charge under the low-user rental rebate scheme. To qualify they must use less than 120 units a quarter.*

Bill Queries

If you have a query, call your local BT office. The number is shown on the front of the bill. You'll be asked for your phone number and connected to the person who deals with your account.

If you are querying the number of metered units the bill says you have used, BT will check the meter readings used to calculate the bill and will also compare the total number of units used with those for previous quarters.

With itemised bills it will be easier to see exactly which calls have bumped up your bill.

If necessary BT will check their record of faults and the meter at the exchange which records your call units. If they find that there's been a fault which has increased your bill they will send an adjusted one.

If you still dispute something on the bill, don't pay for that item until the matter is sorted out. But pay something off the bill and enclose a covering letter explaining why you haven't paid in full.

If you don't pay anything you could be cut off. Then you've not only got the inconvenience of being without a phone but the extra hardship of paying anything from £30 to over £50 (after three weeks) for reconnection.

BT give you only between 35 and 40 days after the arrival of their first bill before they cut you off.

TIP *If you are going to be away from home for a prolonged period during which your phone bill might arrive, tell BT beforehand. Then arrangements can be made so you won't be automatically cut off. This also applies if you or perhaps an elderly relative are going to be in hospital or away convalescing for a prolonged period.*

If you receive a bill that you're sure is wrong, stick to your guns and pay what you'd normally pay. But first check back with previous bills (was there a hiccup once before that turned out to have an explanation?) and make sure that no one could have made an expensive call in your absence without telling you.

Can't Pay?

If you've received a real shocker and can't possibly pay it, tell your local BT office as soon as possible – before you get a final reminder. They may let you pay off the bill in instalments. If they do, start paying as soon as possible. If you can't come to a satisfactory arrangement write to the District Manager whose address should be on the back of the bill.

Still no progress? Write to your local Postal and Telecommunications Advisory Committee, an independent body set up to represent the interests of local customers. Or to the Office of Telecommunications (OFTEL), which is the national independent watchdog organisation set up by the Government to oversee the telephone service after it was privatised. You'll find these addresses at the back of the Phone Book.

Your local Citizens Advice Bureau might be able to help. Or you could write to the chairman of BT, Iain Vallance.

TIP *If you have an elderly or disabled relative or even a neighbour who may have difficulty paying their bills you can act as a guarantor to ensure they won't be cut off. Under the Protective Services Scheme the guarantor steps in as soon as there is a problem and sorts out how the elderly or disabled customer can pay off what's owed. The guarantor doesn't get landed with the unpaid bill but acts as a go-between. For more information about the scheme contact the local head office.*

As a final step, and as an alternative to court action, you can settle disputes through a legally binding arbitration scheme. You pay a registration fee of £15 which is refunded if the independent arbitrator finds in your favour.

All evidence is submitted in writing and the arbitrator's decision is final. If you're not happy with his finding you cannot then go on to take the case to court.

TIP *In cases of hardship it could be worth contacting an appropriate charity, such as those for ex-servicemen and women, to see if they can help out.*

FOUR

Water and Community Charge

Water rates, which used to be the cheapest of all the regular household bills, are due to rise dramatically over the next three years. Users in some parts of the country will see their bills soar by between 48% and 70%. The rises are needed to help pay for cleaning up the environment and improving the quality of drinking water and for investment programmes.

Customers won't necessarily have to swallow the full impact of these increases. You may be able to cut your bills by installing a water meter.

At present the great majority of households are assessed for water rates on the pre-Poll-Tax rateable value of the property. Someone living in a large house pays more than someone living in a small terrace, regardless of how much water they use.

But with the end of domestic rates and their replacement by the community charge the water companies will have to find some other way of deciding how much householders should pay. They have until the year 2000 to find an answer.

One of the most likely methods is water metering – paying a standing charge and then for the amount of water used. Trials which will last three years are going on in 12 parts of the country.

But anyone in England and parts of Wales can have a meter installed now. It costs between £100 and £150 but for some people this will be recouped in a reasonable time through lower water bills.

The people most likely to benefit are those who live in

property which was highly rated where there is only one person or a couple at home who don't use a lot of water.

A meter probably isn't worthwhile where there's a family of four or more who tend to use a lot of water living in a small house. If you are not sure whether you would benefit ask the local water company to advise you.

TIP *Watch out for the sharks! In some parts of the country, doorstep salesmen have been telling householders they will make big savings if they have a meter installed – just to get them to buy one.*

Southern Water estimate that for a year's charges, including sewerage, a person living alone would pay between £40-£60, a couple £65-£200, and a large family £140-£200.

The figures will vary depending on individual use and charges in different areas but they give some idea of how different situations compare.

If you're interested in having a meter installed contact your local water company. They will give you information that will help you work out how much water you use and whether a meter would pay off.

If you decide to go ahead, fill in an application form and either arrange for them to supply the meter or buy one privately but if you do this shop around and compare prices first.

A private company will do the whole job for you. But it might be cheaper to get several quotes from plumbers for installing the meter. Get the water company to check it once the job is done. If there are any leaks you could find yourself paying out for water that is simply keeping your garden – or the foundations of your house! – wet. The water company will also check that the supply isn't contaminated.

Once a meter is installed you can save money by not wasting water. Taking a shower instead of a bath will pay you twice over (you'll save on water heating bills too), and you'll be less likely to leave the garden sprinkler on all day. On the other hand, some people are worried that hard-up families might be tempted to economise too much.

TIP *Under a new code of practice companies will have to pay compensation to customers if they fail to keep an appointment* *or to respond quickly to written complaints or bill inquiries. In certain circumstances they will also have to pay compensation if they interrupt the supply for more than a day without warning.*

Water Bills

Water bills can be paid in instalments by direct debit or by standing order with your bank. If you are an organised person, you'd do better to put so much aside allowing for the annual increases promised for the next ten years – and beyond – in a bank or building society account that pays interest.

The code of practice which is being sent to all householders will explain how to cope if you can't pay your bills.

Community Charge

Almost everyone of age 18 or over has to pay the personal community charge, or poll tax. This replaces the domestic rates and is a new way of helping pay for local council services.

The Department of the Environment estimates that one in four people will be eligible for a rebate. Two kinds of help will be available to those who can't afford to pay:

1. Community charge benefit for people on low incomes. This gives a rebate on what they would otherwise pay.

2. Transitional relief which is mainly available to people whose poll tax in the first year will be much higher than their rate bills would have been. This will only be available until April 1993.

Some help is available for the elderly and the disabled.

Who Can Get Help?

Everyone who is on income support and has to pay the tax can get the maximum – a rebate of up to 80%.

Anyone who gets housing benefit but not income support may get benefit on a sliding scale up to the 80% maximum.

Others on low income (but who may not be getting income support) may also get help.

It will depend on:

- How much money is coming in to you and your partner;

- What savings you both have; if you have £16,000 or more you won't get it.

- How much you need to live on, bearing in mind your circumstances. A large family, or someone who is disabled, for instance, will need more than someone living alone.

If you don't have enough to live on you'll get the maximum rebate. If it's above the minimum you need to live, for every £1 of the amount over, the council will take 15p off the maximum rebate. The final sum – so long as it is 50p or more – is the amount of rebate that you will get.

- The size of the poll tax fixed by your local council.

Under present rules married women can't apply for a rebate on their own account because they are assessed on the basis of joint income. And couples can only claim as much rebate as a single person.

Your local council will work out how much they think you are entitled to. If you disagree you can ask them to look at the figures again. If you still disagree you can ask a local review board to consider your case.

TIP *If you think your income is about to fall and that you'll become entitled to benefit, apply as soon as possible. If you leave your application until your income has dropped you could lose out because benefit won't normally be back-dated. If you know that your circumstances are going to change you can claim up to 13 weeks before the change is due to happen. If you've already paid your whole bill you can still get a refund.*

Most people who need help under the transitional scheme should get it automatically. But elderly or disabled people who didn't previously pay rates or rent will have to apply. Elderly means women of 60 or over and men of 65 or over.

Disabled people are those already receiving certain disability benefits or who are registered blind or are provided with an invalid carriage or help towards a vehicle by the NHS.

You can claim a rebate at any time. Claim if you think you may be entitled to one, even if you are not sure.

The bad news is that the great majority of people, even the

poorest, will have to pay some of the poll tax. Even those getting a maximum rebate will have to pay 20%.

Exemptions

Among the few groups that won't have to pay anything are: resident hospital patients; people who are looked after in residential care homes, nursing homes and hostels providing a high level of care; people who are severely mentally impaired; people suffering from degenerative mental conditions such as Alzheimer's disease; almost all monks and nuns; people with no home who sleep rough; people staying in certain hostels or night shelters; convicted and remand prisoners – except people in prison for non-payment of fines or of the poll tax; volunteers working on low pay for charities; some 18- and 19-year-olds including those in full-time school or further education colleges and some at polytechnics; foreign diplomats and foreign service personnel. Students in full-time education and student nurses who are part of Project 2000 will pay only 20%.

The Collective Charge

This applies to properties where people stay briefly such as some hostels and bed and breakfast hotels. They will have to pay a daily contribution to the landlord who is responsible for paying the charge to the local council.

The Standard Community Charge

People with second homes will pay the personal community charge for the area where they have their main home and may pay a standard charge for the area where they have their other home, provided no one else uses it as their only residence or main residence. If they do they'll have to pay the personal charge instead.

Paying

Normally you can pay a year's charges in ten monthly instalments – 12 in Scotland.

TIP *If you move house tell both local councils or you could find yourself paying the charge on both your present and your former home.*

43

FIVE

Food

Shopping around for the weekly groceries is time-consuming and can be unrewarding. Supermarkets generally have the cheapest prices for groceries because of their buying power and it doesn't seem to matter much which one you use.

A survey published by the Consumers' Association magazine *Which?* in February 1990 found that there's little to choose between many of them as far as price goes. For example, a can of baked beans cost 26p in 111 of the 118 supermarkets they checked. And of 109 prices checked for the same size packs of PG Tips tea bags only 21 weren't priced at £2.37. If you're trying to save money on well-known brands you'll have to hunt high and low for a bargain, they concluded.

Prices varied more between the different supermarkets on foods such as meat, vegetables, cheese and fish. But even if you do make savings on some foods it doesn't mean that your overall bill will be any cheaper, the magazine concluded.

So how can you save on the weekly shop? Here's how:

■ A store's own label products are generally cheaper than the equivalent brand-name products. There may be differences in taste and quality but when you are watching the pennies they can be well worth buying. Give them a try anyway – and note the saving.

■ Buy the cheapest cornflakes, butter, washing powder/liquid or whatever. If you or your family don't like it try the next cheapest until you find something you do like.

■ Buying big can pay off. Larger sizes are almost invariably cheaper than smaller ones – although never take this for granted. Multi-packs can also cost less than single items.

- Buying in bulk is also generally cheaper. But don't get carried away and buy things you can't store properly or that will begin to deteriorate before you've finished them. A sack of potatoes, for instance, can save you £s – but only if you can eat them up before they start sprouting and going soft. Find out if there is a bulk buying group in your area. If not consider getting together with friends to form one.

- Take advantage of special offers for things you normally get. Buy several if you can while the price is low – provided that the special offer really is a bargain. A flash offer of 2p off could mean 2p off your next purchase but you might not discover this until you get the product home and examine the label in more detail.

- Anything sold loose is generally cheaper, weight for weight, than the same thing sold in a packet.

- A whole uncooked chicken is cheaper than buying portions or a ready-cooked bird or cooked portions.

- Don't do food shopping when you're hungry. You'll buy more than you intended.

- Buying fruit and vegetables when they are in season is considerably cheaper than buying produce grown in a hot house or imported out of season. Prices will drop as the season for, say, strawberries, or tomatoes, gets under way.

- Meat is cheaper if you buy when there's plenty about but poor demand. Summer, for instance, is a good time to buy pork, especially if you are buying for the freezer.

- Frozen chickens may be cheaper than fresh birds but they can contain at least 10% more water. Take this into account if you are comparing prices.

- Fresh foods in season are usually cheaper – and tastier – than frozen or canned.

- Streaky bacon is cheaper than back but there is little

difference in the proportion of fat to lean. Bacon bought loose is usually cheaper than when it is vacuum packed and is also less watery. Smoked bacon costs more than unsmoked but it keeps for longer and is better for freezing. Buy cheap bacon pieces for quiches and stews.

■ Collar of bacon makes a cheap and tasty joint. It can be boiled or braised. When cold you can use it in baconburgers, risotto or chopped fine to flavour vegetables, salads or jacket potatoes.

■ Pasta is cheap and versatile. Use it with meat, fish, veg, cheese or eggs.

■ Lentils, dried peas and beans help make a nourishing and filling stew with vegetables and a little cheap stewing meat.

■ White eggs are just as good as brown.

■ Fresh foods approaching their 'sell by' date are often reduced. Think if they can be used in place of something else you had planned.

■ Look out for unit pricing on shelf labels. That shows you the price per ounce, per pound, per gram etc. so you can compare products of different sizes or in different shaped packaging. You can see at a glance whether buying a larger size is saving you money. Sainsbury's have introduced unit pricing for 7,000 items in all their supermarkets.

Although supermarkets have the edge on smaller shops on the price of most of the goods they sell, they can be dearer for fruit and veg. Local greengrocers or markets are often cheaper.

Cut Price Bargains

The time of day that you do your shopping can also save you money. Greengrocers and market stallholders often drop the prices of perishable foods towards the end of the day. Buying late on a Saturday afternoon can bring a big saving. You may even be able to bargain to get a further reduction.

Markets are generally cheapest of all for fresh produce but check the quality. Stallholders naturally display their best produce at the front of the stall. Make sure you get the quality that you want and don't be fobbed off with inferior produce from the back of the stall.

An isolated stall in a tourist spot or outside a railway station might not be so cheap.

While it's a good idea to make a shopping list before you set out and generally to stick to it, allow for some flexibility. Buy useful items on special offer if you can afford to, even if it means going slightly over your budget.

Be prepared to change your menu plans if the main item – such as a joint – is dearer than you'd expected and there's a cheaper alternative. If you'd planned a salad but salad veg are dearer because of the weather or some other factor, look for cheaper alternatives. If lettuce are dear, shredded white cabbage makes a good substitute and grated carrots can replace other veg when they are scarce.

Meat

It's a waste of money to buy meat with a lot of fat on it if you are only going to cut it off or leave it on the plate. But completely fatless meat wouldn't be as tasty and would dry up in cooking. Look for a marbling of fat within the meat, most noticeable in beef, which should provide just enough to give it flavour and to keep it moist.

Don't worry too much about colour. Most people prefer their red meat to be bright red rather than darker because they think it's a sign of freshness. All that it indicates is that the meat has been recently cut. It takes about 20 minutes after cutting for the pigment in the meat to oxidise to a bright red colour. After a few hours some of the surface pigment is affected by temperature and light and begins to turn to a brownish-red colour.

Lean beef displayed in a butcher's shop can vary from bright red to dark red-brown but this doesn't indicate any difference in flavour or tenderness. Dark meat may have come from an older animal but it may not be any less tender.

However, very dark meat could come from a very old animal and be tough with a strong flavour. Or it could indicate that the animal was stressed before it was slaughtered in which case it could lack flavour.

Pork that looks very pale and a bit watery could turn out to be tough.

Cheap cuts of meat can be just as tasty as more expensive cuts if they are cooked in a suitable way. They need slow cooking and moisture. So pot roasting, where the meat is steamed in a pot, braising, stewing or casseroling will bring out the flavour and make the meat tender.

Cheap cuts such as breast or neck of lamb, belly or neck-end of pork or brisket, thin flank, leg, chuck and blade of beef will provide the basis for a nourishing and tasty meal.

Mince is cheap but can contain a lot of fat. Most butchers and supermarkets sell extra lean mince. If you want to be sure about the quality choose a piece of meat and ask the butcher to mince it for you. Or, if you have a mincer, do it yourself.

If you are buying for the freezer, stock up during times of peak supply and low demand. They are: late summer and early autumn for beef, August to November for lamb and the summer for pork and bacon.

Bulk buying should save a lot of money but don't buy more than the freezer will hold (meat on the bone takes up twice as much space as boneless meat) or so much that you can't eat it all while it's at its best.

If you are tempted to buy a side of lamb or pork or a quarter of beef you'll get various amounts of roasting, stewing and braising meat as well as mince, chops and steak. But this isn't a good idea if your family prefers higher quality steaks or chops or for a large family looking only for lower priced cuts.

Recommended maximum storage times for meat in a domestic freezer are: beef – 12 months; lamb and veal – nine months; pork – six months; bacon joints and vacuum packed rashers – three months; mince, offal and sausages – three months. Bacon that isn't vacuum packed will be at its best for only one month.

Fish

To make sure that fish is really fresh check that the eyes are clear, bright and not sunken. The skin should look shiny and moist. Flesh should be firm and have a seafresh smell.

- White fish fillets should be neat and trim and a white translucent colour.

- Smoked fish should have a fresh smoky smell and a glossy appearance.

- Frozen fish should be frozen hard with no sign of partial thawing and with no damage to the packaging.

- Shellfish should be undamaged and closed tightly.

Always check the fishmongers for the best buy of the day. Oily fish such as herring and mackerel are often cheaper than some of the white fish. Ask the fishmonger to fillet the fish for you if they are only available whole.

TIP *Fillets or steaks may be dearer than whole fish but they can work out cheaper because there is no waste. The head and bones weigh heavily.*

Cod and haddock are popular fish but pollack, ling and coley are cheaper and make excellent substitutes. They can be cooked in a similar way. Coley is darker than cod but don't let that put you off. Why pay £2.50lb for cod when you can pay £1.50lb for coley which is just as nutritious?

We tend to think of shellfish as being something of a luxury but some types are cheap. Mussels, for instance, can provide a delicious and economical meal in a few minutes.

Fresh fish should be used as soon as possible. But it can be stored overnight in the refrigerator.

If you buy fish in bulk, either from a freezer centre or super-market or when you're at a fishing port don't buy more than you're likely to eat in the coming weeks. Frozen fish doesn't keep too long at peak quality. White fish and smoked fish will keep for three months, oily fish and shellfish for two months.

Frozen fish is best thawed overnight in a refrigerator. Don't try to hurry up the process by thawing in water. It will lose texture, flavour and nutrients.

TIP *Put pieces of greaseproof paper between fresh fish or pieces of meat such as chops before you put them in the freezer so they'll be easier to separate.*

Fruit And Veg

Take advantage of pick-your-own farms if there's one nearby. The quality and flavour of the fruit and veg will be better than anything you can buy in the shops.

Before you go, telephone the farm to check the prices so you can compare them with what you would pay locally. Make sure that the crop you want is still available. If you are taking children ask what facilities they have for them.

If you want vegetables take a knife or a pair of scissors for cutting, and cardboard boxes to take the produce home in. Farms usually have containers but they can run out.

You may get a discount if you pick at the start of the week rather than at busy week-ends. As the produce is so fresh you can freeze any surplus.

Even if you don't save much on money you'll be treating yourself to really fresh produce – and have an outing as well. But if you're really skint, do your sums first to make sure that it will be worthwhile. Don't forget to add on the cost of the petrol to get you there.

Beware of roadside cowboys selling what seems to be freshly picked produce from a stall. If the punnets are covered in clingfilm, the produce could have been bought wholesale and may not be as fresh as that in your local greengrocers.

Growing your own produce is best of all if you want a truly fresh taste. There's nothing quite like the flavour of a potato freshly dug from the garden or allotment. Or your own newly plucked tomatoes. But before you go seriously into growing your own, consider the cost of seeds and fertilisers.

When there's plenty of cheap fruit about it's tempting to buy it for making jam. But it might be cheaper to buy ready-made. Check the shop prices and work out the cost of your ingredients before you go ahead.

How fresh? Can you tell whether a vegetable is top quality? You can get a general idea about freshness from a glance. But did you know, for instance, that discoloured patches on cauliflower curds don't mar the flavour? Cutting them out is a waste. Or that the stalk of a cabbage is a clue to its freshness?

First class produce not only tastes better but is also more nutritious and better value. Here's what to look for:

■ Broad beans should be well filled and fresh green in colour. The pod should be fairly soft.

■ French beans should be bought young and when snipped the bean should be fresh and juicy. Fine thin ones are usually best although dearer.

■ Runner bean pods should be green and succulent and break easily.

■ Beetroot when it's uncooked should be firm, look fresh and have no fibre or blemished or broken skin. Cooked beets should have skin that rubs off with gentle pressure and be a rich bright red. Over large ones tend to be coarse and lack flavour.

■ Broccoli should be young, firm and fresh.

■ Brussels sprouts can vary in colour from medium to dark green. Look for clean, hard sprouts with no loose or yellow leaves, discoloration or slime.

■ Cabbage. Spring greens and spring cabbage should be bright and crisp looking. Summer and autumn cabbage should be firm, solid and fresh looking. The base of the stalk should be clean and not slimy. Avoid any with insect damage. Winter cabbage should have a firm heart and healthy-looking leaves.

■ Carrots should be well-shaped and smooth-skinned with good colour and free from worm holes and damage.

■ Cauliflowers. Avoid blown, woolly or badly damaged heads. Yellow curds are caused by too much sun or by frost or rain but don't affect the flavour. The base of the stalk should be clean and white. Heads should not be fully developed.

■ Celery should have a smooth, thick stalk, fatter at the base with straight pale green leaves. If the leaves have all been removed it could indicate that the celery is not fresh. Some people believe that celery with the soil attached is best of all.

■ Cucumbers should be straight, large, firm, and fresh-looking with an even colour and no sign of wilting. Avoid any that are very bulbous at one end.

■ Kale leaves should be dark green, young looking and fresh. Avoid any that show signs of damage, decay or yellowing.

■ Leeks shouldn't be oversized or have yellow or discoloured leaves or insect damage.

■ Lettuce should be well-developed, tight and full-hearted with a fresh green colour.

■ Mushrooms shouldn't be dry. Look for a firm cap and fleshy stem.

■ Marrows shouldn't be flabby. Older marrows should be between nine and twelve inches long, firm, in good shape and with a tender skin that has a dull shine. Avoid large marrows which can be coarse and dry textured with a lot of seeds. Marrows should be handled carefully and not put under the weight of other shopping.

■ Onions should be firm and dry with light feathery skins. Don't buy if they are sprouting or are soft.

■ Potatoes should be unblemished with little damage. Avoid sprouting or shrivelled ones or any that are black or green.

■ Spinach. Don't buy if there are brown or yellow leaves.

■ Tomatoes should be firm but not hard. Avoid those that are yellowish in the upper part near the stalk.

■ Apples should be bright, firm and sweet-smelling with no wrinkles or bruises and a good blush if they are red. Surface blemishes shouldn't affect the flavour.

■ Pears are best bought hard and ripened-off at home. They're ripe when the skin yields slightly to pressure.

■ Dessert plums should have a bloom on the skin and be plump, fresh and firm to the touch. Avoid any that are hard or shrivelled or that have poor colour.

■ Bananas are fully ripe when yellow and brown speckles appear on the skin. The flesh becomes sweeter as it matures. Bananas dislike the cold so never store them in the fridge.

■ Choose grapefruit that are heavy – it indicates that they are full of juice. A spongy skin often means thick peel and a small amount of fruit inside.

■ The same applies to lemons. Plump ones that feel heavy for their size and have smooth oily skins have less peel and more juice than large knobbly skinned lemons.

■ Honeydew melons are ripe when they give slightly at the opposite end to the stalk. Galia melons should give slightly when pressed at the stalk end. Canteloupes (including Charentais and Ogen) smell fragrant when ripe and give slightly at the stalk end.

■ Choose healthy-looking, unblemished oranges with a bright appearance. They should not be bruised or wrinkled and should feel heavy in the hand.

■ Pineapples should have a distinctive pineapple smell. To test for ripeness, see if one of the inner leaves of the plume comes away easily.

Choose firm fruit which just gives slightly to the touch, with no blemishes, bruises or soft spots.

Storing up trouble? It makes sense to freeze or bottle fresh fruit and veg when they are plentiful and cheap. They must, of course, be really fresh.

But if you don't organise your storage arrangements you could end up throwing some of it away because it's past its best. Frozen, bottled or canned food is unlikely to go off. But after a time it can lose colour, flavour and some vitamins.

Put labels on your freezer drawers for meat, fish, veg, fruit etc. And keep a note of what's inside on the door.

Date everything before it goes in and rotate the contents so that food that has been in longest is nearest the front, or top of a chest freezer, and will be used up first.

SIX

Household Appliances

You can make big savings by doing a little homework before making any major purchase.

Shops are full of tempting goods with all the latest gadgetry and it's fun to be ahead of the game – to have the latest hi-fi or computer for instance. Salesmen are always eager to tell you about a product's new features. It might be attractive but don't let it sway you unless it will save you money or you had decided to buy anyway.

Let's assume you are thinking of buying a new washing machine or fridge freezer. The questions you should ask yourself (which could apply to many other purchases) are:

■ Will it fit in the space available?

■ Will it do the job I want? Or will I be paying over the odds for extra gadgets I don't really need?

■ Am I buying it at a good price?

■ Will it be economical to run, compared with other models?

■ How reliable is it likely to prove?

■ What does the guarantee promise and what after-sales service will I get?

Once you've the answers to all these questions you are on your way to making a purchase you won't regret.

Here are the points to consider.

Where to Put It

Make sure that whatever you plan to buy will fit comfortably in the spot you have in mind, especially if you are buying a new appliance for the kitchen. A fridge or a cooker that's a fraction of an inch too wide to fit in the space available might just as well be a foot too wide.

If you make a mistake the shop will probably change it or may even give you your money back (although they don't have to) but you're back to choosing something that fits all your other requirements.

With a washing machine, if space is tight you may have to settle for a top-loader which is generally smaller than a front loading machine.

If you're buying a three-piece suite, a three-seater settee might overwhelm your room. If you go for a king-size bed you might discover too late that you can't open the door or wardrobe properly.

The Features

When the sales assistant explains all the features on a cooker, washing machine or whatever, it can sound impressive. But remember that the more features there are the more you are going to pay. So when you've looked at a few models go home and make a list of the features that you really need or like.

TIP *If you want a new cooker and fancy a double oven make a note to check that the main oven will be large enough for your needs. They can be slightly smaller than when there's a single oven.*

The choice can be quite baffling. Microwave ovens, for instance, range from a basic one, with just a clock you turn by hand and a defrost/cook button, to a sophisticated electronic model with touch-pad controls and other features.

Ask yourself:

Do I want all these features? Would I be happier with something that's simpler to operate even if it doesn't have as many functions? Which features will save on the running costs? Do I want stylish extras? Can I afford to pay to have them?

You can buy a cheap washing machine, for instance, from around £190. It will be a basic model with a limited choice of programmes and a relatively slow spin speed so your washing doesn't spin very dry.

Or you can pay between £250 and £350 for a machine that has more programmes and other features including, perhaps, energy saving buttons and a faster spin speed so your washing comes out drier.

Or you can pay £1,000 plus for a high-tech job with all sorts of extras – which you might seldom, if ever, use – and sophisticated looks. Basically though, it won't wash your clothes any better than a machine in the middle price range.

It's a good rule of thumb for most products to aim for a midway price range so that you get most of the features you want without paying more for extras you don't need. Beyond a certain price you really pay for those luxury touches.

TIP *Gas cookers cost more than electric cookers to buy but they are considerably cheaper to run. A pilot light left on, though, can use quite a bit of gas.*

The Price

How much can you afford to pay? With that figure in mind decide on the model you like that fits your budget and compare prices in high street shops, department stores, gas and electricity showrooms (if they sell what you're after) and mail order catalogues. Look out for sales and special discounts and don't be afraid to ask if you can have it cheaper if you pay cash.

A Mean Machine Or An Energy Guzzler?

With anything that runs off electricity the price you pay for it in the shop is only part of the cost you have to consider. There's also the running cost.

New appliances are cheaper to run than old ones so if you buy new to replace a machine you've had for years it should save you money from the start.

Some appliances use more electricity than others. And some manufacturer's products are greedier than others. It isn't easy to sort out the mean machines from the guzzlers.

The idea of 'energy labelling' so shoppers can compare running costs has been around for years. Ten years ago the Department of Energy published a paper proposing that water heaters and domestic appliances such as cookers, fridges, freezers, washing machines, TVs, dishwashers and tumble driers should carry labels showing their energy consumption in standard tests. The proposal is still sitting in somebody's in-tray.

TIP *A cylinder vacuum cleaner uses less electricity than an upright.*

Appliances that use a lot of electricity – although they may be used for only a short time – include, in order: an electric shower, electric cooker, immersion heater, electric fire, washing machine, tumble drier and dishwasher.

Products that use electricity at a slow rate include electric light bulbs, TV, hi-fi, fridge, freezer and vacuum cleaner.

But appliances that don't use a lot of electricity can still add significantly to your bill when they're on for long periods. So a freezer which has to be switched on all the time can be the second most costly appliance (after a cooker) that's contributing to your bill.

TIP *A chest freezer uses slightly less electricity than an upright. The smaller the freezer the less it costs to run.*

Most washing machines have some form of economy programme, so you can use less water (a half load programme) or heat the water to a lower temperature. There can be big differences in the amount of water various makes use.

TIP *An electric overblanket uses twice as much electricity as an underblanket.*

Although some appliances have energy labelling, others don't so it's difficult to make comparisons between different makes. The John Lewis Partnership include energy labelling on all fridges and freezers that they sell, showing how much each model is likely to cost to run for a year.

Appliances made by manufacturers that belong to the Association of Manufacturers of Electrical Domestic Appliances (AMDEA) are more likely to have energy labelling than cheap imports.

One source of comparative running costs is the Consumers' Association magazine *Which?* They regularly test appliances and often include comparisons of running costs. You may be able to get back numbers in your local library.

TIP *A toaster doesn't use a lot of electricity and it's cheaper to make toast this way than to use the grill.*

How Reliable?

Some types of product are basically more reliable than others. Unless you are unlucky you shouldn't have to worry too much about: upright freezers (generally the most reliable of all domestic appliances), chest freezers, fridge freezers, tumble driers, microwave ovens, vacuum cleaners or colour TVs.

Washing machines then dishwashers are more likely to go wrong than most other domestic equipment, according to an annual survey carried out by the Consumers' Association. The good news is that they are getting more reliable.

They found that video recorders needed more repairs than TVs but not as many as dishwashers and washing machines. *Which?* lists those makes which are most reliable and those which are more likely to let you down.

As a rough guide to reliability see how long a manufacturer is prepared to guarantee a product. But you would need to check exactly what is being guaranteed.

TIP *An automatic washing machine is cheaper to run than a twin tub.*

Guarantees And After Sales Service

When you pay a lot of money for something, you hope it's going to give you years of service. And so it should.

Nevertheless it can be reassuring to have the manufacturer's guarantee – just in case. This usually covers parts and labour for at least a year. When it comes free with the product it's an added bonus. You might as well fill in the registration card and send it back if required. Keep the guarantee and your receipt together in your filing system.

If you've been unlucky and bought a rogue product you should claim from the trader who sold it to you. He is legally responsible and should give you your money back or, if you wish, a replacement.

But sometimes you run into problems. The trader may have retired and closed the business or gone bust. If the problem is small or you bought your purchase from a trader a long way away, you may feel it would be quicker and easier to claim on the manufacturer's guarantee.

Read the terms carefully, especially the small print. Some guarantees expect you to pay the postage, transport or even labour charges involved in repairing or replacing parts. Others are for such a short period – maybe just three or six months – they're hardly worth having. Some don't cover the problems most likely to occur.

A good guarantee won't short change you on any of these points and may even cover the product for up to five years. If you like everything else about it, it could even be the bonus that persuades you to buy that particular brand. It shows that the manufacturer has faith in the reliability of the product. You get peace of mind at no extra cost.

But because the situation with guarantees is so confusing an attempt is now being made to bring in a standard guarantee that is easy to understand.

In addition to the manufacturer's normal guarantee, customers are often invited to take out extended warranties, protection plans, service contracts or insurance contracts when they buy a big electrical product.

TIP *A washing machine that heats up only cold water will be more expensive to run overall than one that takes some hot water from your system. If you've gas central heating the saving will be bigger.*

With an extended warranty you pay a one-off fee when you buy and the original manufacturer's guarantee is extended for between three and four years. If you are thinking of taking one out, read the terms carefully and check to see if there are any exclusions.

With maintenance contracts you pay a certain amount each year which covers the appliance for free parts and labour and may also include a regular service. These provide more comprehensive cover than extended warranties and cost more.

They are all sold to give you 'peace of mind.' Are they worth it?

Sir Gordon Borrie, the Director General of Fair Trading,

says that while some might be worthwhile others are simply a selling ploy and a means of putting extra money in the pocket of the trader.

The Consumers' Association says they are poor value for money and that you would be better off paying for repairs as they arise. But if your machine is used heavily you may feel it's worth having an extended guarantee just for the peace of mind.

A better idea, the Association suggests, would be to work out what your repair bills would be likely to come to in a year and put so much aside each month in an account that pays interest to cover the cost as it arises.

Spare Parts

You can get some indication of how long things are expected to last by the length of time that manufacturers guarantee to supply spare parts.

The code of practice of the Association of Manufacturers of Domestic Electrical Appliances (whose members include all the big UK manufacturers) gives minimum times for which manufacturers and importers should keep functional spare parts for various products.

From the time they stop making a model the code says they should continue to supply functional spare parts for a minimum period, as follows:

■ Small appliances such as kettles, toasters and irons – five to eight years;

■ Cleaners, direct acting space heaters, spin and tumble driers, wash boilers – eight years;

■ Cookers, dishwashers, washing machines, water heaters but not immersion heaters – ten years;

■ Thermal storage space heating – 15 years.

The code says this should be the bare minimum and that, in practice, manufacturers and importers should carry spares for much longer.

For non-functional parts – those that affect the appearance rather than the running of the product – spares should be available for all discontinued models of domestic electrical appliances for at least four years.

The code doesn't include TV sets but British manufacturers say they keep spares for most colour TV sets for at least five years after production ceases.

Parts for discontinued models of gas cookers should be available for between ten to 15 years.

These are minimum periods so if you buy a new model washing machine made by a member of AMDEA that stays in production for say, five years, parts should be available for at least 15 years altogether.

TIP A vacuum cleaner that gets blocked by fluff uses more electricity. Emptying it after each use saves money.

Buy or Rent?

Most people rent their TVs or videos because they want the reassurance that they will be repaired free of charge if they break down, or be replaced if necessary. But these products are generally reliable and surveys show that you'd be better off buying in most cases.

However, there's a good case to be made for hiring expensive items that you don't have room to store or that you only use occasionally such as DIY or garden equipment or a video camera that you might want to use for a wedding or holiday. Radio Rentals hire out a range of domestic products including washing machines, dishwashers, washer driers, tumble driers, and video cameras.

It could be worthwhile if your appliance has broken down and you're in for a long wait while it is repaired, or if you have an influx of visitors.

Read the conditions carefully and check on the position over insurance and repairs. There's usually a penalty if you don't return the article on time.

SEVEN

Cut Price Shopping

You can buy most things for less than the going price if you are prepared to give a little time to it. Even if you're pushed for time it's always worth shopping around – perhaps by phone – to find the best deal.

The Sales

Stores' regular sales are the most usual place for bargain hunting. Because they are now held so regularly throughout the year it's worth waiting for the sales for most major items you have to buy as well as for regular household things that need replacing such as towels and bedding.

It's easy to get carried away and to fritter money. So before you start out make a list of the things you need and be prepared to stick to it. Work out how much you can afford to spend. You may see all sorts of 'bargains' that you think will come in handy. The chances are they won't.

Go at the start of the sale so you can have your pick of what's on offer.

Think big. You'll make a bigger saving if you buy something like a good winter coat than if you buy a cardigan. But a big price reduction doesn't necessarily mean that the item is a bargain. It may have been over-priced to begin with. So keep in mind that vital question; is it good value?

Some goods are specially bought in for the sales and are marked 'Special Purchase'. You may find what you want among them but be on your guard. Some of the stuff can be rubbish.

With clothes, avoid extreme fashions, way-out colours or anything that might be out of date within a few months. Go for classic lines and colours that don't date.

Check the care label. A dress that can't be washed and has to be dry cleaned isn't much of a bargain, especially if it's light coloured.

TIP *It's illegal to put up a sign that says sales goods can't be exchanged or money refunded. If you buy something that's faulty and you weren't warned about the fault and couldn't have spotted it, you're entitled to your money back. You have the same rights when you buy at any other time.*

Try out zips, and check whether the garment is supposed to have a belt. If you are buying separates make sure that both pieces are the right size. If you can't try a garment on check the size on the label – it might not be the same as the one on the hanger.

Some of the biggest bargains are in electrical appliances. Look for showroom or demonstration models that have been reduced because of a minor chip or scratch. If it's a demonstration model at least you know that it works!

But make sure that it has the features you want, that it will fit in the space available in your kitchen and, most important, that it's not an energy guzzler but will be cheap to run.

If something is marked 'seconds' or 'damaged' try to find out what's wrong. If it's not obvious ask the assistant.

TIP *If something is marked 'imperfect', 'seconds' etc. you can't expect it to be as good as the perfect version. But the fault should be minor and the article capable of doing what you'd expect from it. A washing machine may have a dent or scratch on the paintwork but it should work properly. If it doesn't you are entitled to your money back if you report the fault at once. But you're not entitled to your money back if the fault is something you should have spotted.*

You can get excellent bargains in crockery and glass 'seconds'. These are usually manufacturers' rejects that have such a slight flaw that you may not be able to detect it. It could be a slight variation in pattern or colour that only an expert examiner can spot. You can get top quality products for half price or maybe even less.

But watch crockery or glass that is marked "end of line" or

"end of range". You won't be able to replace breakages.

If you are planning to switch from sheets and blankets to a duvet, sales are a good time to make the change.

There are often big reductions on slow-moving lines such as canteens of cutlery and luggage – worth considering if you are likely to be looking for a wedding present in the near future or if your luggage is falling apart.

TIP *Take advantage of 'price promises' where a store offers to match any lower price charged by other stores in the neighbourhood for the same item. It's a sign that prices should be low. But if you find what you've bought at a cheaper price elsewhere tell the store and ensure that they keep their promise to refund the difference.*

Markets

Street and indoor markets have bargain basement prices for fruit and veg, clothes, some household wares, flowers and plants and many other goods.

Stallholders can afford to charge less than supermarkets and high street shops because they have lower overheads and can buy from a variety of cheap sources.

Although most things will be cheaper don't assume that everything will be – and watch the quality. Fruit and veg, for instance, might be quite ripe and not suitable for bulk buying. A cheap toy might break the first time it's played with.

TIP *It's worth haggling to see if you can get something off the price.*

You can usually rely on stallholders who have a regular pitch. If something isn't up to scratch they'll generally give you your money back or offer an exchange.

But beware of characters who set up a temporary pitch with a tressle table. And never fall for the sales patter of men who sell from suitcases. They may be selling stolen or counterfeit goods and if anything goes wrong you won't find them again.

Check the labels on clothing to see if it's a reject. Sometimes the labels are cut off.

If the stallholder tells you it's Marks and Spencer stock – at 'half the price' – it could be a reject from the factory that makes for Marks and Spencer. But it isn't good enough to meet their standards so look carefully for faults. It may be something quite slight such as a pattern flaw that isn't really obvious or missing buttons. Or it could be a major defect such as one arm longer than the other or serious stitching or seam faults.

TIP *Check the size of a garment in case it's got the wrong size label. Try it on if you can. If you can't, then make a note of the stall number so you'll know where you bought it in case you have to take it back.*

Other points to watch:

- Expensive items, such as top brand names in perfumes, watches or sportswear being sold cheaply could be either stolen or counterfeit. If it's stolen the police may ask you to hand it back and you'll get no compensation. The only exception is if you bought at a 'market overt'. These are old-established markets set up by Royal Charter. If you buy something there and didn't know it was stolen you're considered to be the legal owner. The local council's markets officer will tell you if you bought from a market overt.

- Cut-price jewellery may not be all that's claimed. If it's a precious metal such as gold, silver or platinum look for the hallmark. Ask the stallholder to give you a receipt with a description of what you've bought. If he's reluctant don't buy. If you later suspect that you've been sold a phoney, report it to your local Trading Standards office.

- Examine cheap toys carefully to make sure they're safe. Check they don't have sharp edges or parts that could easily come off and be swallowed by a child.

Give a gentle tug to the head and limbs of a doll to make sure they're secure. Then give the doll a gentle shake. If it rattles there are probably small bits of plastic left over from the manufacturing process inside. They can look like sweets and a child may be tempted to swallow them if they get out. If you buy anything unsafe report it to a Trading Standards office.

- Check the date-marking on food to see that it's still fresh.

■ Don't get carried away by the trader's spiel. To make you think you're getting a bargain he may say something is worth a lot more than it is, then bring the price down to what may seem to be a give-away. Don't fall for it. If it is really a give-away price it will probably go to friends of the trader's planted in the crowd. He wants you to think he's got bargains you can't resist. Show him that you can.

Your Rights

When you buy from a market you have the same rights as when you buy from a shop. If something has a significant defect you're entitled to your money back provided you return it promptly. But you're not entitled to a refund if the fault was pointed out by the trader or if it is one you should have spotted before you handed over your cash.

If you can't find a stallholder ask for the name and address of the company running the market or see the market superintendent in the local council offices. Market traders have to be licensed by the local authorities who keep a record of names and addresses.

If the trader refuses to give you your money back contact your local Trading Standards office.

Car Boot Sales

You can find big bargains at a car boot sale provided you get there early enough – and that usually means turning up about an hour before the stated opening time. Even so you are quite likely to find dealers have got there before you and have soon snapped up the best bargains. But that can still leave lots of goodies, especially if you are looking for something a little off-beat or to fill a particular spot in your home.

Many stallholders are householders who have had a clear-out and are getting rid of things they no longer need. Often they are in the process of moving house.

Because they are more interested in getting rid of stuff than in making a fortune they pitch their prices low. Usually you can bargain for an even lower price. If you turn up late when they are thinking of packing up they may be willing to sell things for next to nothing just to get rid of them.

Some large-scale car boot sales are semi-professional events with dealers mixed in with the private sellers. You'll generally pay more and find fewer real bargains at these events. A small car boot or table sale, perhaps organised by a local organisation, is likely to be more rewarding.

When you buy privately you have fewer rights if your purchase turns out to be useless. And at these events you might find it harder to trace the seller.

Auctions

You need to know what you're buying at an auction. You may have only a limited opportunity to test things out and your rights are more restricted than with other forms of selling.

The Conditions of Sale which may be posted up in the saleroom or printed in the catalogue usually say that neither the auctioneer nor the seller are responsible for the genuineness or condition of the goods on sale. Unless you could prove to a court that they acted unreasonably you have no come-back if you buy something that turns out to be a load of rubbish.

Cars are sold cheaply at auction but you can't test drive them to see how they run. So they're a gamble even if you have an engineer to look one over for you.

You're also up against experienced dealers.

If you want to buy something like a piece of furniture or a picture you may find you have to buy things you don't want to get something you do want.

Charity Shops And Nearly New Shops

If you want to freshen up your wardrobe with something new and the pennies are scarce you can often pick up excellent bargains in a Charity or Nearly New shop. At one time they were thought of as just one step up from a jumble sale – all right for a hippie teenager but a no-go area for mum. But many are now patronised as much by the bargain-hunting well-heeled as by the down-at-heel.

The smarter the area, the smarter the goods in the shop. With dresses, coats and suits going for just a few £s they represent great value – if you don't mind wearing someone else's cast-offs.

Generally the shops only accept clean, good quality clothing and articles. Often they're almost new. They can be great hunting grounds for children's clothes – and for presents.

Second-hand Shops

These are more commercial and may specialise in furniture, bedding, clothes, bric-a-brac, or a mixture of everything.

The goods are cheap but that doesn't necessarily mean that they're inferior. Only a few years ago antique dealers wouldn't have looked at the sort of heavy oak furniture that used to be found in homes everywhere in the thirties. Then it became collectable and shot up in value.

Furniture that looks shabby can often be transformed with DIY renovation and a good polish. If you like the general shape of a piece of furniture or are attracted by the wood or material it's made of it's worth considering whether you could do it up. Don't waste your money though if it looks like a job for a professional.

Be wary of electrical goods which could be dangerous, and of upholstered furniture which could be a fire hazard. It's almost certainly filled with inflammable foam that could give off lethal fumes if a flame was dropped on it.

All new upholstered furniture sold in shops now must by law be covered in flame-resistant material or contain a flame-resistant lining. It's illegal to sell the old dangerous type, even in second-hand shops, but Trading Standards officers are still finding it on sale. So take care.

Bucket Shops

These are agencies that sell flight tickets on charter and scheduled services at heavily discounted prices. They advertise in the holiday pages of national newspapers and magazines.

Savings can be dramatic and some people who use them regularly never consider paying full fare.

Phone round for the cheapest prices but if they sound too cheap there could be a snag. When you arrive at the airport you might find that the ticket isn't accepted, and when you try to contact the agent he might have vanished.

When you are phoning, get full details of the airline, the airport and the time of the flight. Before you pay for your ticket check that the flight you are booked on exists and that you are really booked on it. When you reach your destination make sure that you are booked on the return flight.

Buying Privately

Sooner or later you can find almost anything you want in the small ad columns of your local newspaper or specialist magazine. In some parts of the country free papers are published weekly that carry nothing but advertisements. Postcards displayed in the windows of small shops can be equally rewarding.

When you buy something privately you have fewer rights if anything goes wrong than when you buy from a trader. Some traders try to cash in on this by advertising in the small ads columns and pretending to be private sellers. This is illegal and publications often carry a warning notice pointing this out.

You can sometimes spot suspect ads when you see the same telephone number repeated in a number of advertisements. A trader who is pretending to be a private seller could be trying to get rid of things he wouldn't risk selling in his business.

The law says that goods sold in the course of trade must be of merchantable quality and fit for their purpose. If they aren't the customer is entitled to a refund. But when a private individual sells something, it doesn't have to be of merchantable quality or fit for its purpose. But it must be accurately described.

So you need to ask a lot more questions when you buy anything privately. Ask if it works well and how long the seller has had it.

If possible, get the seller to give you a demonstration so you can see that it works. If it's making odd noises you'll know there's something wrong.

If you wait until you get home to try out your purchase and then find it doesn't work you've no come-back unless the seller described it wrongly. Take someone with you to act as a witness to what is said and maybe jog your memory over points you should check. If you're buying something technical and you are not very knowledgeable take an expert who can examine it for you.

Often articles are advertised with a price followed by the letters o.n.o. which stand for 'or nearest offer'. Even if it doesn't say this, offer less and be ready to bargain.

Jumble Sales

They used to be a joke but any young mum strapped for cash who can pick up a pram, in perfectly good order for between £5 and £10 and maybe a set of baby clothes for less than a £1 doesn't think they're particularly funny.

The better the district and the more worthy the organisation running the sale, the better the 'jumble'. Seasoned attenders travel miles to get to a jumble sale in an exclusive area. Apart from good quality everyday wear, they often pick up designer-label clothes for around £2 or £3.

You need to be there very early to get to the start of the queue. Even then you could find yourself behind dealers and gypsies who are very quick to home in on the best bargains.

One Day Sales

These are often advertised at short notice and appear to offer fantastic bargains. They are sometimes conducted as mock auctions, which are illegal. At these sales the bargains go to people planted in the audience. You could end up with a load of rubbish and no way of tracing the people running the sale. By the time you find out the true value of what you've bought they're miles away conning another lot of punters in another town.

Not all one day sales are rip-offs but you should be extra careful before you hand over your cash. Never buy anything you haven't examined and make sure you get a receipt with the traders' name and address on it.

Tips! Tips! Tips!

- Collect discount stamps that retailers are giving away free.

- Catalogues and discount shops generally offer very

competitive prices. They can keep them low because their operations are less labour intensive. Other retailers often use the prices charged in a catalogue shop such as Argos as a benchmark in deciding where to pitch their prices.

■ Buy on your credit card providing you are sure you can pay off what you owe at the end of the month. That way you keep money in your account earning interest for an extra five to eight weeks.

■ Take advantage of holiday discount schemes such as Air Miles. Companies taking part award customers so many free air miles in return for spending a certain amount – perhaps one mile for every £10 spent. Air miles can be redeemed for either a free flight or a package holiday. But don't be tempted to overspend just to clock up Air Miles!

■ Other businesses running holiday discount schemes include: Barclaycard, American Express, Girobank Travel Connection Service, TSB Trustcard Travel Club, Midland Discount Holidays, Skipton Building Society Travel Club, and Chase Travel Club.

■ Countdown is an organisation that offers discounts to members in 14,000 stores, some restaurants, hairdressers, car maintenance centres, theatres, holiday tour companies and financial services. Members pay £15 a year and can get discounts wherever the red and blue Countdown sign is on display. On joining they receive a set of discount guides, membership cards for themselves and partner and a quarterly magazine. The organisation guarantees all discounts.

It could pay off if there is a selection of Countdown businesses in your area and you are likely to use them fairly regularly anyway.

Details from : Countdown 88/92 Earls Court Road, London W8 6EH (Tel. 071 938 1041).

■ Enter competitions. The more you enter the greater your chance of winning something, especially if there are a lot of prizes for the runners-up. Practice writing tie-breaker slogans that often decide the winner. Magazines are published regularly giving details about competitions and tips on how to win.

Keep Well, Look Good

How often do you come out of the chemist's amazed at how much you've spent on everyday items?

A pack of plasters, hairspray, talcum powder, cotton wool, handcream, toothpaste, a new cosmetic brush, eye shadow, a box of tissues are all small items but, added up, they can take a significant bite out of your weekly spending money. And if you get a cold or flu or some other complaint your bill can rocket, whether you are buying on prescription or over-the-counter remedies.

You can trim the bills by:

■ Looking after your health so you don't fall victim to a host of minor ailments;

■ Not buying proprietary products that you don't need – however glowing the publicity;

■ Asking your chemist for the cheapest product that will do the job.

Try to get into the habit of taking a brisk 20 to 30 minute walk – longer, if you can manage it – every day. It will not only help keep you fit and better able to resist minor illnesses but you'll feel good too. Try to walk at a speed that leaves you slightly, but only slightly, breathless.

Get out into the sun whenever you can (but don't overdo sunbathing). The ultraviolet rays react on the skin's surface oils to produce vitamin D which is important for bones and teeth and gives you energy.

Regular exercise classes or swimming are excellent ways of keeping fit. It's been claimed that keeping fit may add ten years to your life. It will certainly put more life into your years! You're less likely to suffer ill-health from heart disease, bone disorders (such as osteoporosis), depression and mental disorders and even conditions such as diabetes.

Diet too is important. Eating plenty of fresh fruit and

vegetables (not overcooked and not stored for too long) will do more for your skin than many beauty products. Buy what's in season and cheap. Even in the middle of winter, root vegetables are cheap and plentiful. You get lots of vitamins from raw vegetables such as cabbage, cauliflower and salads, citrus fruits, such as oranges and grapefruit, and tomatoes.

If you eat a balanced diet you don't need to buy expensive vitamin supplements unless you are in the 'at risk' group which means the elderly, pregnant women, schoolchildren, convalescents, people on special diets and those on low incomes.

Don't buy pills that claim to relieve stress. They won't. Avoid foods that you know can make you unwell. If you have a tendency to headaches, for instance, try to avoid stressful situations and skip the foods that might trigger one such as chocolate, cheese, coffee, tea and Chinese foods. Alcohol, especially red wine, beer and sherry can bring on headaches in some people.

If you need to lose weight, eat less but make sure you eat a variety of foods. Cut down gradually starting with the foods that you know are going to put on unwanted inches such as chocolate and pastries. If you're in the habit of piling food on the plate try eating from a smaller plate.

Get sufficient sleep – but not too much, especially if you're prone to headaches.

Colds

Coping with a streaming cold is not just miserable it can also be a pain in the purse.

By the time you've bought something to fight it off, and then something to ease your sore throat, aching head, stuffy nose and hacking cough you'll have spent a fiver or more. None of these remedies will help you get better any quicker. At best they can help you cope with the miseries by relieving symptoms. But when you see what they've cost, you may feel even more miserable!

If you're thinking of buying a proprietary brand ask the chemist if there is an unbranded BP equivalent available. BP products must comply with the standards of the British

Pharmacopoeia and are often cheaper than branded versions.

Here are some other cheap and cheer-you-up ways of cutting the cost:

■ To clear a stuffy nose put a towel over your head and inhale the steam from a basin of plain hot water. Add menthol, eucalyptus oil or something similar if you prefer.

■ To ease aches and pains and any fever take soluble aspirin or paracetamol.

■ Pastilles and lozenges containing honey, sugar and glycerine and maybe antiseptic and a little anaesthetic can help ease a sore throat. But swallowing a spoonful of runny honey or sucking ordinary sweets or chewing gum will help too although they are no better for your teeth.

■ Instead of buying an antiseptic gargle or mouthwash, gargle and swallow soluble aspirin in water. Remember to include this aspirin in your total dosage.

■ Get plenty of rest, especially when you first feel the symptoms coming on.

■ Take lots of hot drinks. They'll make you feel better.

■ Try grandma's favourite remedy – a hot toddy at bedtime. To a glass of hot water, add a spoonful or two of sugar to taste, a few cloves, a slice of lemon and a measure of whisky.

Other homely remedies you might like to try include:

Tying an old sock round your neck with the foot at your throat. It shouldn't be one you've washed!

Give your feet a mustard bath.

Chop and boil onions, add salt and pepper, drain well, add a lump of butter and eat.

Put a dessertspoonful of honey, juice of a lemon and a knob of butter in a pan, bring to the boil, and drink as hot as you can.

Prescriptions

.Prescription charges are now so high that it's worth checking whether you can buy the same thing – or its equivalent – over the counter for less.

If you're suffering from a minor complaint, see if your local chemist can recommend medication. But don't let fear of high prescription charges put you off seeing the doctor if you're ill.

If you think you are going to need regular prescriptions it may be worth getting a 'season ticket'. You can apply for one from your local family practitioner committee.

Dentists

The less treatment you need the more you'll save. You can do something about this by cutting down on sugary foods and drinks and by regularly brushing your teeth. This helps fight gum disease and decay.

If you can't resist sweet things it's better for your teeth to eat them all at once rather than to nibble away throughout the day. Saliva helps break down the sugar but it doesn't have a chance if you keep popping sweet things into your mouth.

To make sure you don't pay more than you need:

■ Check whether you are entitled to free treatment;

■ Make sure that you're getting NHS treatment. Confusion over whether treatment was on the NHS or private can prove costly. Clear this up for every fresh course of treatment;

■ Don't break appointments without notice – dentists can charge for loss of time.

Beauty

When you are buying cosmetics and toiletries look for the cheapest you can find and give them a try. If you or your family don't care for them try the next cheapest until you find something that's reasonably priced and will do the job. But don't skimp too much. Shampooing your hair in washing up liquid, for instance, isn't going to do it much good.

Many supermarkets sell own brand toiletries, such as toothpaste, soap, shampoo, tissues and make-up that are cheaper than the proprietary brands.

Larger sizes are generally cheaper than smaller ones. (You

can see this at a glance when products are unit priced.) Sachets of shampoo, for instance, are an expensive way to buy, although useful if you're going to be washing your hair away from home. A family-size bottle of shampoo should be best value.

There are lots of different types of shampoo for various conditions of hair. A mild one won't damage dry hair and anyone in the family with greasy hair can use it more often.

Look out for special offers or the chance to buy two of anything for the price of one or three for the price of two.

Cheap skin-care products can do what you need as well as the more expensive ones, although they might not smell as nice. In tests, women who put an expensive moisturiser on one side of their face and a cheap moisturiser on the other for a week – and didn't know which was which – were as likely to prefer the cheaper one. So start with the cheapest until you find one you like. Try it on a less obvious part of your neck first in case you are allergic.

You can pay extra for the luxurious way some beauty products are packaged. Generally, the less packaging, the cheaper the product will be.

Save on hairdressing bills by getting a good cut that you can wash yourself. When you go to the hairdressers don't be persuaded into having extras you don't really want or need.

Sometimes salons have a cheap day, usually early in the week. There may be special rates for pensioners or students.

EIGHT

Car and Travel

Nearly 15% of the average weekly income goes on motoring and fares. Every year the bills get bigger. It's tempting to assume that there's not much you can do about them short of selling the car and giving up long distance journeys.

There are less drastic ways, however, in which you can keep costs down.

Economy Driving

You can save on petrol and wear and tear on your car with the AA's six-point fuel saving plan.

- Accelerate gently and smoothly through the gears and avoid harsh braking;

- Use the highest gear possible under prevailing conditions. Cruise whenever possible. Don't labour the engine;

- Turn the engine off in traffic jams that look like lasting;

- Use the choke only when necessary and for the shortest possible time;

- Ensure that your car is properly maintained – that timing, plugs, points and carburettor are spot on and brakes are not binding;

- Make sure that tyre pressures are correct.

There are various devices you can buy which claim to save fuel but the most effective economy device in any car is the driver's right foot.

This was proved during organised fuel economy runs using standard production cars, say the AA. While some of the techniques used in these events may not always be practical in everyday motoring they are worth keeping in mind. In more detail this is what they recommend.

Avoid fast starts. Grand Prix get-aways use 60% more fuel than slow smooth ones.

Within practical limits the higher the gear, the less the amount of fuel used to maintain a given speed.

Get into top as soon as the engine will pull smoothly – lower gears use up to 50% more petrol. An optional overdrive unit may be a worthwhile investment in cutting petrol consumption if you do a large annual mileage.

Push the choke in as soon as possible after a cold start. If you keep it out too long it not only increases fuel consumption considerably but causes undue engine wear as it washes away the protective oil film on the cylinder walls.

Hard acceleration and braking waste petrol. Think of the accelerator as a petrol tap: the more you open it the more fuel you'll use. Using a wide open accelerator to pull from 20-40 mph in top gear uses more petrol than cruising at 60 mph.

The faster you go the more fuel you use. Driving at 70 mph you can use twice as much petrol as at 35 mph. But smaller engined cars have a wider range of consumption than larger ones. So with careful driving you can make bigger fuel savings on smaller cars than larger ones.

In general you'll save most on fuel by cruising at around 40 mph. Fuel consumption is highest in low-gear low-speed traffic such as you get in busy towns and cities. Moving forward in a queue of cars at 10 mph uses twice as much petrol as cruising at 35 mph in top gear.

TIP *Try to maintain a steady speed in top gear on moderate hills. If you have to change down, use the minimum throttle opening to make the climb at a reasonable speed.*

TIP *Don't rush up to obstructions and road junctions and brake sharply. Allow time to make changes in speed as gradually as possible. Sudden variations in speed are wasteful.*

Tyre pressure has a small but significant effect on fuel consumption. The higher the pressure the lower the rolling resistance of the tyre and the better the fuel consumption. So it pays to ensure that your tyres are inflated to the car maker's recommendations and are not allowed to run under-inflated. But don't exceed the recommended pressure significantly or the handling of the car can be seriously affected.

Regular maintenance and correct tuning are essential to get maximum economy. If you're not sufficiently expert, leave engine tuning to your garage.

TIP *Shop around for petrol. Service stations at supermarkets may be the cheapest. When the Consumers' Association carried out a survey of petrol prices around the country three quarters of their volunteer researchers found at least 8p difference in leaded four star petrol by shopping around in their own area. A quarter found differences of between 15p and 22p. If you bought 30 gallons a year and your car averaged 30 mpg, a difference of 8p a gallon would save you £24 over the year.*

Using the correct grade of petrol for your car is one of the simplest and most efficient ways of keeping down fuel costs.

Check what octane rating or star grading the manufacturer recommends and decide which grade and brand you can use without getting engine 'knocking' – a sign that you're using too low an octane rating.

Some petrol stations have petrol blending pumps which dispense a range of octane number blends within each star rating at slightly differing prices. This gives a finer selection in deciding the most suitable grade.

Servicing

It's a false economy to delay getting a car serviced beyond the time recommended by the manufacturer or, worse still, not to get it serviced at all.

To keep costs down, carry out a few simple checks yourself between services so that you can prevent unnecessary wear and tear and tackle problems before they go too far.

Even if you're not very handy you can;

■ Regularly check the tyre pressures, including the spare. Check the tread depth and look for wear and tear. Uneven wear usually means there is a problem somewhere: let the garage investigate.

If a tyre needs replacing shop around among tyre specialists for the best price. If you wait until the car goes in for a service and ask the garage to do the job you may have to pay more.

■ Keep an eye on fluid levels in the radiator, battery, engine oil, brake and clutch fluid reservoirs. If you find one has dropped suddenly it could indicate trouble. Get it checked immediately.

■ Look out for rust spots and treat them as soon as they appear with a recommended treatment.

■ If you have any problems with lights, horn, washers or wipers and you can't deal with them yourself get the garage to see to them immediately.

■ Put in anti-freeze before the temperature drops.

The Garage

Finding a reliable garage isn't always easy. Ask around among friends and neighbours, especially those who have the same make of car as you. If your car is under a manufacturer's warranty go to an authorised dealer or the warranty may become invalid.

TIP *You have more protection if you use a garage that belongs to a trade association (you will be protected by a code of practice) or is recommended by the AA or RAC. If you can't see any signs or logos on display ask if they are members of a trade association, such as the Motor Agents' Association.*

Don't feel you have to stay with a franchised garage once the warranty has expired. You might do better with one that friends recommend and that may be closer to home.

Look for premises that are clean and that seem well organised and where the staff are friendly. It helps if they display prices for standard services so you have some idea how much you are going to pay before you collect your car.

When you are getting an estimate for a repair job make sure it includes labour, VAT and the cost of materials. When you take your car in for a service or repair tell them exactly what you want done. Put it in writing if possible.

If it's a service make sure you know beforehand what it includes. Tell the garage if you want the manufacturer's recommended servicing schedule to be carried out and agree items – if any – that can be left out.

If it's a big job get a quotation (which is a fixed price) or an estimate (a close guess) beforehand. Check that labour, parts and VAT are included. If you don't want the job to go over a certain limit tell the garage they must get your permission before they carry on. Leave your phone number.

Find out how long the job is going to take and get a set time for collection. Make sure you get a detailed invoice showing all the work carried out, parts and labour costs. Check that they've done the work agreed and query anything that you don't understand.

TIP *Cheap second-hand tyres can be dangerous. A survey carried out by West Yorkshire Trading Standards officers in their area found that one in three second-hand tyres on sale was dangerous and unfit for road use.*

Problems?

If the bill is sky-high or you think the garage has done a poor job talk to the manager or owner right away. If the problem can't be sorted out you'll probably have to pay up to get your car back. Write to the garage owner or manager saying that you are dissatisfied and that you've paid 'without prejudice'. Keep a copy of the letter.

Then take up your complaint either with your local Trading Standards officer, the consumer adviser at your local Citizens Advice Bureau, or, if the garage is a member, the AA, RAC or trade association.

If you don't find out that there's something wrong until you've driven the car away take it back at once and tell the garage that you're querying the bill and the work.

TIP *The cheapest car for replacement parts, according to the Consumers' Association, is a Mini. Among other small cars the Citroen 2CV6 and the Fiat Panda are reasonably cheap while most superminis and cheap family cars costing up to £6,500 also have cheap parts.*

Selling Your Car

You'll get a better price selling privately through a small ad in the local paper, a postcard in a shop window or in a specialist car magazine or trade paper. If you are buying a car from a trader it's simpler to trade in your old model but you're unlikely to get such a good price.

You can sell at an auction but you have to pay a selling fee plus a percentage of the selling price.

Spring is the best time to sell if you can manage it. After the winter doldrums people start to look around for a car they can have in good time for the summer.

Try to avoid selling after the new registration date on August 1. Lots of people who've bought cars with the new registration letter will have sold their old cars in part exchange or will be selling them privately. There are so many second-hand cars around that prices inevitably dip and you might have to wait a long time for a buyer.

You're unlikely to get such a good price either when interest rates are high. People stuck with sky-high mortgage repayments are unlikely to take on anything extra – especially if they have to buy on credit. You'll probably have to drop your price and may have a long wait before you find a buyer.

Some people trade in their cars after two years. But if you like to stick with your vehicle then you should consider selling before it reaches the stage where it starts to need major repairs. This is generally between four and six years for a car with average mileage of between 40,000 and 60,000.

You can get some idea of what price to ask through car price guides you can buy in the newsagents and by looking at advertisements to see what other sellers are asking for cars of the same make, model, age and condition. Be prepared to knock something off your asking price.

Ask for payment by a Banker's Draft if possible. If you do accept a cheque don't hand over the car until the cheque has been cleared.

Buying A Car

If you're looking for a new car and have decided on the model you want, shop around for a discount. Make sure you are comparing the on-the-road price. See how much each garage is offering for your old car.

You should be able to get a bigger discount at the time of year when trade is slow. Winter is a good time (although not so good for selling your old car) or just before the new registration letter comes in on August 1.

Most new cars lose a third or more of their value in the first two years: check in motoring magazines which makes and models hold their value best. Because cars lose so much of their value in the early years you are really better off buying a car that is one or two years old.

You will be offered a warranty by the manufacturer with your new car and may be invited to take out an extended warranty too. Check carefully what it covers. They usually lay down conditions which you must keep to if the warranty is to stay in effect. Don't commit yourself until you've had a chance to examine whether it's going to be worthwhile or whether you wouldn't be better off putting the extra money you would pay for the warranty into an interest-paying account at the bank or building society.

Used Cars

You can buy a second-hand car from a private individual, from a trader or from an auction.

If you buy privately you have less legal protection if the car turns out to have hidden faults than if you buy from a trader. The law says that a private seller mustn't give wrong information about the vehicle. A trader, on the other hand, must not only give an accurate description of the car but must sell you one that is of merchantable quality – that is fit for its purpose.

There are, however, lots of tricks that rogue traders get up to. The most common is turning back the mileometer so that the vehicle appears to have done a lower mileage and be worth more than it is.

You can often buy more cheaply at an auction but you have no chance to try the car out beforehand and no come-back if it's a let-down.

Unless you know the car and its owner, buying a second-hand car is a gamble. You can reduce the odds by taking along a mechanic friend to look at the car for you or by asking the AA or RAC to carry out an independent inspection for a fee.

The AA's service is limited to members only, the RAC's is available to anyone although non-members pay more. You'll have the reassurance that you're not buying a tarted-up heap and the seller should have no objection if he's got nothing to hide. He might even be prepared to share the cost of the inspection with you!

Ask to see the servicing record, the vehicle's registration document and if the car is more than three years old the MOT certificate. See if the car matches up. If the seller hasn't got the registration document – he may say it is with the DVLC at Swansea – don't buy.

If he does hand over the registration document make a note of the name and address of the last owner and check with them that the mileage is correct. You could also ask them about the car's history.

If you've any doubts don't buy. If you do decide to buy try haggling over the price.

TIP *A trader might offer you a credit deal but you don't have to take it just because you are buying from him. You might be able to get a cheaper deal through a bank, building society or finance company. Leave a deposit on the car while you shop around. Make sure you get a receipt with the words 'deposit subject to inspection'. If an inspection then reveals faults you should have no trouble getting your deposit back.*

Travel

Coach It's much cheaper to travel long distance by coach than by train. With reclining seats, on-board toilets and a hostess service providing food and drink – available on the inter-city routes – it can be a comfortable way to get from one city to another at often half the cost of going by rail.

Competition between the coach companies helps keep prices down. You might not always find a coach going to the destination you want at the times that you want to travel but there are few places they don't go to.

National Express operates Britain's largest network of express coach routes with daily services to around 1,500 destinations in England and Wales and, through Caledonian Express, Scotland. Many of their airport services run every two hours, providing bargain travel for holidaymakers. Between Birmingham and London coaches depart every thirty minutes.

The main drawback of coaches is that they can get snarled up in heavy traffic in the big cities.

National Express have various discounts. Men and women over 60 and holders of the Young Person's Discount Coach card can get one third off the normal adult fare. There's a low price discount card for visitors to Britain and special cut rates for people travelling as a group.

From time to time they have 'special offer' fares which are advertised locally.

Bus In London 70% of travellers use cards or passes that give some sort of discount on the regular fares for buses and Underground trains. Visitors to the capital can also benefit.

If you are visiting the city or having a day out, and have several journeys to do, a one-day bus pass which costs £2.30 for journeys in Inner London and £2.60 for all zones, may save money. (The cheapest bus fare is 30p for up to one and a quarter miles outside central London and 50p for journeys up to three quarters of a mile in central London. On the Underground the cheapest fare outside the central zone is 50p, and inside 70p.)

A one-day Travelcard which can be used on the bus, Underground and BR in all zones can also save you money if you have to do several journeys. This also costs £2.60 for adults, 90p for children aged between five and fifteen.

In many towns men over 65 and women over 60 are entitled to a free bus pass.

Train Travel-happy pensioners have journeyed all over Great Britain for a few £s on British Rail's occasional special discount fares. Watch out for advertisements.

For people of all ages, railcards can also cut the cost of train travel. They are discount cards issued to people in certain categories. Some can't be used during the rush hour.

They include:

■ Senior Citizen Railcard. Available to men and women aged 60 or over. It costs £16 for a year and knocks at least a third off most BR fares. Savings are bigger if you travel at off-peak times.

■ Family Railcard. Available to anyone over 18. It costs £20 a year and gives adults half price or one third off standard class (what used to be called second class) travel with up to four children under 16 travelling for £1 each.

There must always be a child in the party and at least one adult who is named on the railcard. Adults and children do not have to be related to one another. The card can be bought in the names of one or two adults: either or both holders plus up to two other adults can each travel at a discount so long as at least one child travels with them. You can only buy standard class tickets with it.

■ Young Persons Railcard. Available to anyone under 24 (or mature students in full-time education). It costs £16 a year and allows one third off standard class rail travel including Savers and Cheap Day Returns. Holders must pay certain minimum fares that apply up to 10 am on weekdays most of the year.

■ Disabled Persons Railcard. Available to the severely disabled. Your local station should be able to tell you exactly who qualifies. It costs £12 for a year and entitles the holder to between a third and half off certain fares.

Adults who accompany the disabled person travel at the same reduced rates.

■ Network Card. Available to any adult in the Network SouthEast area which, despite its name, goes as far north as King's Lynn and as far west as Exeter. It costs £10 for a year (£5 for anyone over 60 or who already holds a Young Person's Railcard) and saves a third on the normal price of adult tickets.

The same saving applies to up to three adults travelling with you, while up to four children aged between five and 15 can travel at a flat rate fare of £1 each. A second person can be named on the card and use it. Limited to travel within Network SouthEast after 10 am weekdays and at any time on Saturdays, Sundays and Bank Holidays.

■ Network Gold Card. Annual season ticket and London Travelcard holders in Network SouthEast are issued with Gold Cards which entitle them to buy tickets for leisure journeys (those after 10 am on weekdays or anytime at weekends or bank holidays) at one third off normal adult leisure fares. They can also get reductions off one day Travelcards and other bonuses.

Many of these cards will have paid for themselves after just one or two journeys. So they are well worth having if you are likely to make several train journeys in a year, especially if any are likely to be long ones, and you are eligible.

TIP *When rail fares are going up buy a season ticket just before the increase if you can and for as far ahead as you can. If your employer doesn't give season ticket loans as a standard perk try asking. If not, will a member of the family lend you the money?*

Saver fares can make dramatic savings on InterCity journeys to and from London if you avoid the rush hour.

A return ticket can work out at half or less of the standard rate. A Blue Saver saves you most. You can travel any day of the week except Friday and certain days over Christmas. A White Saver can be used any day of the week. If you have a railcard you can get a third off the Saver fare.

Groups can get a 25% discount if there are at least ten in the party. Sixteen or 17-year-olds in the party can travel at the Child fare rate which qualifies for the 25% reduction.

If you have to change trains on the journey the reservation carries forward to the second train. Reservations in first class cost £2.

Adventurous young people set on seeing the world can buy an Inter-Rail ticket which allows anyone under 26 up to one month's unlimited travel in 22 countries in Europe and the Mediterranean. It costs £155 and there are various additional discounts.

NINE

Repairs

Getting anything serviced or repaired these days is a major expense. High call-out charges make anyone hesitate to ask a repairman to come to the house to do a repair.

Just to get a mechanic to look at your washing machine can cost £14 plus £4.22 for every ten minutes after that. Outside normal working hours you're likely to be making a minimum payment of £18.18.

Sometimes you've no choice. If your pipes have burst you need a plumber. If gales have ripped tiles from your roof you want them replaced before the rain gets in.

If you're very lucky you will have a reliable handyman you can call up who'll do the job quickly and at reasonable cost. But if you don't have such a treasure maybe your friends or neighbours know of one. A local builders' merchant or Home Improvement Centre may be able to suggest someone. Check around before you resort to the Yellow Pages.

In an emergency try to limit the damage so you don't have to call someone out during unsocial hours and pay double or triple rate for it:

■ If a pipe has burst, turn off the supply at the stopvalve. It's often, but not always, close to the kitchen sink. Make sure you know where it is. If escaping water cannot be immediately controlled turn on all the cold water taps to drain the pipework and storage system quickly.

Turn off central heating and switch off the immersion heater.

■ You might be able to bind the burst pipe with tape, old towels or polythene as a temporary measure.

■ If a pipe freezes, turn off the main stopvalve. Check whether the pipe has split. If it has, empty the cold water storage system by turning on taps and flushing the WC. Thaw the pipe by applying hot water bottles, a thick cloth soaked in very hot water or with a hair dryer. Never use a naked flame.

■ If your washing machine is overflowing turn off the water supply to the machine. It should be on the pipework near the machine. Check that the hose hasn't become disconnected. If you can't get water to flow into the machine it could be because the hose has kinked.

■ If the lights have failed check with your neighbours to see if there's a local power failure before ringing the electrician.

■ If your radiator has suddenly gone cold it probably needs bleeding. This is something you can do yourself.

■ If your central heating boiler isn't working check that the thermostat is at a sufficiently high setting and that the time switch is on the 'on' period. If you're on gas, see if the pilot light has gone out and simply needs relighting.

■ If it's an appliance that's gone wrong check with the instruction book.
Make sure you've switched it on. If that is not the problem, disconnect the appliance before you do anything else to it. Then check that all parts are connected, that the plug is correctly wired and that the fuse has not blown. Fuses can blow after a while for no particular reason. Keep spares available so you can replace a fuse with one of the same amps.

■ If you suspect the electric socket isn't working, test it by plugging a different appliance in.

■ If you've been burgled and don't know where to start on emergency repairs, call your local Victim Support group.
If you've a good neighbour or friend living near by, call them in before you call in the professional. There may be a simple explanation that you've not spotted. Or they might have enough skills to deal with the problem for now.

You can save quite a bit on repair bills by learning how to do it yourself at local evening classes. Many local authorities run classes in subjects such as car repairs, home maintenance, plumbing, decorating, brickbuilding, plastering and carpentry.

Every job you can do yourself will cost a lot less than if you had to call in the professional. You'll make the biggest savings with jobs that take a long time such as decorating or that involve hefty call-out charges or where labour charges are high.

At the classes you not only get expert tuition but can swap ideas with other students and pick up tips.

For convenience it's handy to buy everything under one roof which you can do at a DIY superstore. But although competitive, they aren't necessarily cheapest for everything. A builders' merchant might be best for basic building materials and they will generally cut things to size for you – a service you are unlikely to get at other outlets.

High street chains such as Woolworth are competitive for painting and decorating materials.

TIP *Is there a hire shop in your area? It may pay you to hire expensive equipment that you won't need often.*

It's generally not a good idea to attempt DIY gas or electrical repairs. When a fuse keeps blowing it may be because there's a fault in the wiring or in a fitting and that's better left to a qualified electrician.

And while it's useful to be able to do basic plumbing repairs, uninformed tampering with plumbing and heating services can cause serious damage and lead to expensive repair bills. Everything connected to the water supply has to comply with the Water Byelaws.

But if you think you're skilled enough to repair a domestic appliance, write to the manufacturer and ask for the servicing manual for the machine. Some may not like you to have it on the grounds that if you do the job badly it could be dangerous.

TIP *If you are on good terms with your neighbours, consider swapping DIY skills. They may be a dab hand at painting and decorating while you may be a whiz mechanic. You could also share emergency tools. You, for instance, might have the* *drain-clearing rods while they have the plastic sheeting for covering holes in the roof or broken windows.*

Be Prepared

You can avoid that panicky feeling by taking a few precautions beforehand:

- Get to know the layout of your house. Find out where the mains switches are so you know where to find them if you have to turn them off.

- Try to find a reliable plumber, electrician, builder etc. for normal maintenance work and keep their phone numbers handy for emergencies. When friends recommend someone add them to the list.

- Keep anything you might need in an emergency such as a torch, candles and matches, waterproof tape, insulating tape, fuse wire and fuses, a spanner, hammer and screwdriver somewhere where you can easily find them.

- Once every six months clean out the waste pipes from the sink and basin with a rubber plunger. Never put untreated melted fat down the sink. It will harden in the pipe as it cools and finally cause a blockage. Regular use of undiluted household disinfectant may remove accumulated grease from a waste pipe.

- Check your cold water storage system from time to time. If it is metal, look for signs of corrosion on the underside – brown and white spots and patches. Call the plumber.

- Regularly check the condition of hosepipes on plumbed-in washing machines. Vibration can cause flexible connections to fracture and leak.

- When the central heating is off during the summer, switch it on occasionally to keep the pump running smoothly. Turn radiator valves once or twice a year to keep them moving freely.

- Don't wait until winter before attending to dripping taps

and overflow cisterns. Even the occasional drip can block a waste or overflow pipe with ice overnight and cause flooding inside the home.

■ Maintenance contracts, where a manufacturer or retailer agrees to maintain and repair your appliance in return for an annual fee can save you a lot of worry. The Consumers' Association does not consider them to be a good 'buy'.

Cowboys

Cowboy operators are always on the look-out for likely victims. Here are common types:

The Inventor He calls round to say that he was just passing your house and noticed something wrong in your roof area. He may suggest it's slipping/damaged/broken/or missing tiles/ a wonky chimney pot/broken guttering or anything else that he thinks you can't easily check out for yourself. He offers to repair it there and then. There's no harm in thanking him for the information but get someone reliable to check out if anything really is wrong and, if necessary, put it right.

The Knocker He calls by, says your drive is cracking up and offers to resurface it cheaply if you pay something/all in advance. He may take your money and vanish or, if he does return, he'll do such a poor job that you'll have to get someone else in to do it again.

The Eel He's a close relative of The Knocker. But this slippery customer accepts cash to lag your pipes and makes such a rotten job of it that, come the winter, they burst.

The Time Waster He promises to get the job done quickly but doesn't turn up for months. He does a quick job and maybe charges a cheap price but again makes such a mess of it that you have to get another firm in to put it right.

You should never fall for these tricks but, in any case, never pay in advance (unless it's a major building job where the builder may need some payment to buy materials) or until you're satisfied with what's been done. And never sign a satisfaction note saying you are satisfied with the work that has been done until you've had an opportunity to test it out.

Assuming you haven't got the name of a builder, plumber or electrician to hand, how can you avoid being ripped off by a cowboy?

You'll reduce the chances if you shop around. Get quotes from at least three repairmen if you can. They might not be able to give you a complete figure until they can see what has to be done but you should get some idea and can compare their call-out or minimum charges.

If the fault is in an appliance, the manufacturer's own engineers or their authorised engineers should be approached first. Or you might be able to get a repairman to come from the shop that sold the appliance to you.

Otherwise ask the repairman if he belongs to a trade association. Many have codes of practice which provide protection for customers if there's a dispute.

TIP *A call-out charge usually covers the first 15, 30 or 60 minutes of work. After that you'll pay more. So don't waste the repairman's time – and your money – with unnecessary chat or encourage him to chatter about things not connected with the job he's doing.*

Useful Trade Organisations

Association of Manufacturers of Domestic Electrical Appliances, Leicester House, 8 Leicester Street, London WC2H 7BN. Most British manufacturers belong. Code covers repairs or servicing done by them or by their service agents. It sets standards for speed and quality of service, guarantees on paid-for repairs and runs conciliation and arbitration schemes to settle disputes.

Radio, Electrical and Television Retailers' Association, RETRA House, 57-61 Newington Causeway, London, SE1 6BE. Lays down standards for the sale and servicing of electrical and electronic goods. Has customer conciliation panel for disputes.

Institute of Plumbing, 64 Station Lane, Hornchurch, Essex RM12 6NB. Registered plumbers must be experienced and have proved their competence to the Institute. Their Business Directory of Registered Plumbers is held at many public libraries. Or you can get a list of registered plumbers in your area by sending them a stamped addressed envelope. Investigates complaints against registered plumbers.

Confederation for the Registration of Gas Installers, St Martin's House, 140 Tottenham Court Road, London W1P 9LN. Registered installers' work is inspected before they join and regularly monitored afterwards.

National Federation of Roofing Contractors, 24 Weymouth Street, London, W1N 3FA. Has 6,000 members nationwide who are all experienced contractors. Runs an arbitration service.

The Heating and Ventilating Contractors' Association, ESCA House, 34 Palace Court, London W2 4JG. Representing central heating contractors. They vet members' work and guarantee against faulty workmanship. Will provide names of members in your area.

The National Inspection Council for Electrical Installation Contracting, Vintage House, 36-37 Albert Embankment, London, SE1 7UJ. Registered electricians have passed an exam and have their work inspected and equipment checked. Investigates complaints against members.

Federation of Master Builders, Gordon Fisher House, 14/15 Great James Street, London WC1N 3DP. Runs warranty scheme.

Building Employers' Confederation, 82 New Cavendish Street, London W1M 8AD. Runs a guarantee scheme aimed at driving out the cowboys.

Area electricity companies have a code of practice. It recommends that:

■ Repairmen call within three working days;

■ 80% of jobs should be completed on the first visit;

■ The remainder of the work should be completed within 15 working days;

- You should be offered an appointment on a particular day and preferably told whether it will be in the morning or the afternoon;

- You should be told of any minimum charges when you call.

TIP *Check whether damage caused by an emergency is covered by your household insurance. Contact the company immediately. Insurance companies usually agree to you going ahead with emergency repairs but will want estimates for more substantial repair work. Some insurers operate a 'hotline' service for emergencies which puts you in touch with approved repairmen in your area.*

You'll probably still get best value from an established local one-man or family business with a reputation to maintain, low overheads and who won't charge you for travelling time.

Choosing a repairman from the Yellow Pages or from a card dropped through the letter box should be a last resort unless you know something about them that gives you confidence.

It's better to wait, if you can, until a repairman you know or who is recommended can get around to you (if he's busy it's probably because people know he is reliable) rather than taking a gamble on the unknown.

Other Ways To Save On Repairs

You can save on shoe repairs by:

- Putting stick-on soles on newish shoes that have leather soles. If you do it yourself make sure the sole is not too heavy for the shoe. Don't wait until they are thin;

- Having toe caps fitted as soon as you notice the soles getting thin towards the end. They cost little and add a lot to wear;

- Getting minor repairs done. Stitching, seams, buckles, bows and eyelets are all repairable and can add months to the life of your shoes. Damaged zips in boots can also be replaced;

- Regular cleaning. It may be a chore but it keeps the uppers flexible, reduces cracking and helps keep the rain out;

- Not wearing the same shoes every day. Wear them

alternately with other pairs.

If your shoes need major repairs find out how much it is going to cost before going ahead. As a rough rule of thumb, if the repairs will cost one third or less of the price of the replacement it is worth having them done. If it's going to cost more than that you're better off buying another pair.

Never dry wet shoes by a fire, radiator or hot pipes. Stuff them with newspaper and leave to dry at normal room temperature. Using shoe trees or, alternatively, newspaper stuffed inside when they're not being worn, will keep the shape longer. Scuffed heels or uppers can be given a new look by painting them with liquid paint sold in shoe shops and repairers.

Cut down on dry cleaning bills by washing delicate woollens, velour, lace, and silk garments by hand in a cold or cool water washing liquid. With silk, test-wash one corner first to make sure the colours aren't going to run.

Washing is not suitable for heavy velvet, satin, crepe silk or bulky items such as overcoats which should be dry cleaned.

Cut down on laundry bills by treating stains immediately. You can buy stain removers in the shops. Stain Devils that deal with specific stains are particularly useful to have by in an emergency.

If there's nothing handy and it's a non-greasy stain, washing in cold water might do the trick (hot water might set the stain and do more harm than good.) Otherwise sponge with a weak solution of washing-up liquid and warm water.

Salt sprinkled on blood, red wine or deep fruit stains will absorb the moisture and some of the colour. But if the fabric is delicate take it to the dry cleaners as soon as you can.

TEN

Insurance

With most things you buy there's something to see for your money. With insurance you are buying peace of mind. That isn't much consolation when it's time to pay the bills, especially if you've never had to claim.

But it's false economy not to insure or to under-insure your possessions. Equally, don't pay more than you need.

With something like insurance it can be tempting to stick to the same insurance company that your parents deal with. Or to pay up automatically when the yearly reminder comes through the letter box. But it's sensible to shop around.

The cheapest insurance isn't necessarily the best but there can be very big differences between what one company charges you and what another will charge you for the same amount of cover. To find the best deal you should:

- Work out what cover you need;

- Get quotes from several companies;

- Make sure the policy you decide to take out will pay out in all the circumstances you want covered. To do this you'll have to read the policy document.

It might be tedious but it is a legal document and the company will only pay up in the circumstances described in it. Don't rely on the salesman's word for what cover you have.

Remember many life insurance salesmen work on commission. They'll probably tell you all the plus points of the policy they are trying to sell, but not what it doesn't cover.

- Never be bamboozled into signing just to get rid of a persistent salesman. With something like life insurance it can cost you dear if you change your mind at a later date and try to end the policy early.

Deciding What Cover You Need

There are two main types of insurance:

General insurance covers you against accidents or loss – damage to your home, a car crash, burglary or perhaps something going wrong with your holiday.

Life insurance is taken out on your life and pays up either at a specific date or when you die.

■ If you own or are buying a house you need house building insurance.

■ Whether you own or just rent your home, you should insure your possessions against loss, damage or theft.

■ If you own a car or a motorbike you must have insurance by law.

■ If you go on holiday you should take out cover.

■ If anyone would suffer financial hardship because of your death you certainly need life cover.

If you already have all the insurance cover you need, make a note of when each policy is due for renewal. Some weeks ahead study it to see if it really covers all you require. Look especially at any exclusions: it may exclude something you want covered.

Getting Quotes

You can shop around in three ways:

■ Do it yourself by ringing round likely firms for a few quotes. It's better to choose a firm on a friend's recommendation than simply to go by an advertisement.

■ Ask your bank manager for advice. If he can't help, he can put you in touch with one of the bank's insurance experts.

■ Ask a registered insurance broker to help. You can find a broker through the Yellow Pages or by contacting the British

Insurance Brokers' Association (Tel. 071 623 9043) who will send a list of members in your area.

TIP *Registered brokers look at the whole market and see what best suits your requirements. They are bound by law to put your interests first and are governed by a code of conduct. You don't usually pay them a fee. They get commission from the insurance company they introduce you to. Someone who calls himself a 'consultant' is unlikely to be a registered broker and may be selling insurance for one or more particular companies.*

Get quotes from several companies. Ask if there are any discounts. Some companies offer special rates to people in certain jobs or trade unions; to non-smokers; people of a certain age, such as over 55; or, in the case of house contents insurance, where security devices have been fitted or you are a member of a neighbourhood watch scheme.

If you decide to renew your existing policy consider whether there have been any changes in your circumstances since you last renewed it. Maybe you can get a cheaper premium because you've installed locks to your windows or a burglar alarm?

It's important when renewing a policy to tell the insurance company about any changes in your circumstances during the year.

When you take out a new policy you must tell the company anything that might affect any claim you might make in the future, especially about any criminal offence, however minor.

Some of the biggest complaints from policy-holders have arisen because a company has refused to pay out on the grounds that the policy-holders didn't disclose all relevant facts about their circumstances. The best policy is to tell them everything you can think of that might remotely affect a claim.

Exclusions

Even the most expensive policies don't cover everything. Generally, the more you pay in premiums the fewer exclusions there will be.

If when you read the policy you discover that it doesn't cover a particular situation that you want covered, talk to the broker or insurance salesman about it. You may have to pay a little extra to get it included, but there's no point in having insurance if it isn't tailored to your needs.

Most people don't look at the small print of a policy until they have a burglary, lose or break something, or have an accident. It's only then that they discover, perhaps, that their cover isn't as full as they assumed. So study the policy document carefully for what it doesn't cover. Ask about anything that isn't clear or that you don't understand.

House Contents

Whether you own your home or rent it you need insurance protection for its contents. If you are burgled or your possessions are damaged you can claim for loss or for repair.

What they cover Most policies cover furniture, furnishings, household goods, kitchen equipment and other appliances, food and drink, televisions, videos, computers and audio equipment, clothing, personal effects and valuables such as jewellery and personal money up to stated limits. In fact all the things in your home, garage and outbuildings you would take with you if you moved house but not fixtures and fittings or boats, caravans and cars.

The risks they cover You're usually covered for loss or damage by fire, theft, lightning, escape of water from tanks or pipes, oil leaking from fixed heating systems, storm, flood, subsidence, heave or landslip, falling trees or aerials, riot or malicious acts, explosion, earthquake, impact by aircraft, vehicles or animals.

Breakage of mirrors, glass-topped furniture and fixed glass in furniture is usually included. Some policies also include accidental damage to televisions, videos, home computers and audio equipment.

Companies are very specific about what they do and do not insure. For instance, they generally won't pay up on a theft claim if you have lent or let your home, or part of it, unless there is a forced entry.

They may put a limit on the value of a piece of jewellery or work of art or even a video. There is generally an overall limit to all these valuables but the company may raise it if you ask and give them full details.

TIP *If you lose your key and decide to change the locks it can be quite an expense. Some policies cover you for this.*

There are two types of home contents insurance:

■ The cheapest is indemnity insurance where the company pays the cost of repairing damaged articles or of replacing what has been stolen or destroyed, less an amount for wear and tear and depreciation. Because it's cheap it's attractive but it's only the second-hand value that's covered and you could have to pay out quite a bit if you have to buy a new replacement.

■ New-for-old policies cost more but are probably a better bet. They pay the full cost of repairing damaged articles or of replacing them with new if they've been stolen or destroyed with no deductions for wear and tear or depreciation.

Furniture, carpets, domestic appliances, televisions, videos and audio equipment can normally be insured on a new-for-old basis but not usually clothing and household linen.

You can take out a standard policy to which you can add on 'extensions' such as accidental damage. You might want to be able to claim, for instance, if someone knocked a bottle of red wine over your best new cream carpet.

Or you can have an all-risk policy. This gives you a high level of cover but is the most expensive and will still have some exclusions.

Assessing your worth It's up to you to decide on the value of your possessions. You could have a shock when you add up how much it would cost to replace them at today's values. But if you don't bother to work out their value and to keep the figure up to date – unless you have a new-for-old policy – you are selling yourself short. If you valued a ring at £30 ten years ago and never updated it to today's value, £30 is all you'd get.

To work out the value of the contents of your home go from room to room, including the loft, and work out how much it would cost to replace each item new at today's prices. Even with a new-for-old policy there will usually be some items, such as clothing, and household linen, which are covered on their second-hand value only. Deduct something for wear and tear and depreciation on these items. You don't have to make a deduction for things that don't suffer wear and tear such as a wall mirror.

Make a chart with a column for each room. Down the side, list your main possessions and fill in the boxes with your estimate of their value.

Add up the figures. With a new-for-old policy the total is the sum you need. With an indemnity policy add a suitable allowance for inflation over the next five years.

The Association of British Insurers, at Aldermary House, Queen Street, London, EC4N ITT, have a sample check list you can use for guidance.

You can avoid a DIY assessment of your worth with what's known as a 'hassle-free' or 'fixed sum' policy where an assessment is made on certain factors such as how many rooms your home has. A fixed amount of cover is suggested.

Building Insurance

You must have building insurance if you have a mortgage and it is essential even if you don't. Your home is the biggest investment you've got and paying for repairs can cost a fortune.

But some policies may not be giving the cover you need which could cost you dearly if you made a claim, while others may be giving you cover you don't need and for which you are paying extra.

To find out if you are getting good value from your insurance, read what the policy says. See what it covers and what it doesn't cover.

TIP *Look out for companies that offer no claims discounts.*

Property has to be insured for what it would cost to rebuild it – not the market value. If you under insure, the insurance company may not pay up even though the claim is for something less than total rebuilding.

What they cover Policies vary in the cover they provide and in their terms and conditions.

Most insure the structure, permanent fixtures and fittings,

such as sanitary fittings and permanent kitchen and bedroom cupboards, and interior decorations.

They generally also include garages, greenhouses and sheds.

The risks Most cover damage to your home by fire, lightning, explosion, earthquake, thieves, riot and malicious persons (such as vandals), storm and flood, aircraft or things falling from them, subsidence, landslip and heave, falling trees, impact by vehicles or animals, breakage or collapse of TV aerials, escape of water from tanks or pipes, and oil escaping from fixed heating installations.

They also cover you for: the cost of alternative accommodation if your home is so badly damaged that you can no longer live in it; property owner's liability (you could be liable, for instance if a tile fell off your roof and damaged someone else's car. You would mainly be covered for this under your home contents insurance but your buildings policy covers you if no one is living in your house or if you've let it to tenants); underground service pipes and cables and indoor glass such as windows and skylights and baths, washbasins and W.C.s.

Check your policy for what it doesn't cover. This may include damage by storm or flood to fences and gates, or by frost, sonic bangs, and contamination by radioactivity from nuclear fuel or waste.

TIP Older houses which are likely to have relatively shallow foundations and which were built on clay can be vulnerable to subsidence after a long spell of drought. But the worst culprits can be thirsty trees such as willows, oaks and poplars.

Most policies say that you will have to pay something towards the cost of some claims. It may be for certain types of damage such as storm or flood damage or the escape of water from tanks or pipes. Almost all policies say that you must pay something if the damage was caused by subsidence, landslip or heave. This is usually a specific amount such as £500 but it may be a proportion of the cost of rebuilding your home.

What's it worth? The rebuilding costs of your home should include an allowance for permanent fittings such as central heating and additional charges which could be involved in rebuilding such as demolition costs and professional fees.

You may need a surveyor or architect to make the valuation for you. Or you can get some idea from the leaflet 'Buildings Insurance for Home Owners' available from the Association of British Insurers, Aldermary House, Queen Street, London EC4N 1TT.

Car Insurance

There are three basic types of car insurance:

■ Third party is the cheapest. It covers liability for injuries to other people including passengers; for damage to other people's property; for accidents caused by passengers; and liability arising from the use of a caravan or trailer attached to the car.

■ Third Party, Fire and Theft costs about 10-20% more. It also covers fire or the theft of your car. If the car isn't kept in a garage at night theft cover may be excluded or subject to special conditions.

■ Comprehensive is the most expensive but it covers a lot more including: accidental damage to your own car even if the accident was your fault; personal accident benefit in the event of death or permanent disablement of the policyholder; medical expenses up to a stated limit; and loss or damage to personal effects in the car up to a stated limit. Some policies will pay out on extras such as the cost of hiring another car while yours is being repaired. Two out of three owners have comprehensive cover.

TIP *Most policies cover the policyholder while he is driving someone else's car. But cover is limited to Third Party only, even with a comprehensive policy. So you wouldn't be able to claim off your policy if you accidentally damaged a friend's car you'd borrowed. Make sure the owner has comprehensive insurance which covers you as an alternative driver under the terms of his policy. Then if you damage his car, he can claim off his insurance.*

If you've got an old banger worth only a few hundred pounds the extra cost of comprehensive cover can be almost as much as the car's worth. So you may be better off insuring it for Third Party Fire and Theft, especially if the driver is under 25 and paying a high premium.

Cutting the cost You can keep the cost down by agreeing to certain limitations, by opting to pay an excess, or by getting a special discount.

Look out for deals that offer:

■ Lower premiums if you agree to limit the driving to yourself and maybe also to a named individual. But only do this if you're never going to let anyone else drive your car.

■ Discounts for two-car families where both cars are insured with the same company.

■ The opportunity to pay a 'voluntary excess' which means you pay the first part, which may be £50, of any claim.

■ Discounts for special category such as motorists aged 55 or over or a woman driver.

All companies offer a no-claim bonus if you don't make a claim. Scales vary but usually they range from 30% for one claim free year up to 60 or 65% after four or five years. No claim discount protection is often available for motorists with maximum discount. By paying a little extra on the premium a number of claims are allowed without loss of discount – typically two claims in a three or five year period.

These are all attractive options worth considering. But they are only part of the policy. Like any other kind of insurance you have to look for the one that suits you – and your pocket – best.

Whether you are taking out motor insurance for the first time or your policy is due for renewal, shop around. Get quotes from several companies and read the policies to see what they offer – and what they don't cover.

Look for the policy that offers most cover at the least cost. Try to find out how well the company handles claims. This isn't easy but ask around among friends in case they can recommend a company that's given them good all-round value and no hassles when they make a claim.

TIP *If a car isn't in a roadworthy condition the insurance company might not pay up on a claim.*

You may also be able to reduce your premiums by:

■ Switching to a smaller, less powerful or even an older car. Family cars with moderate repair costs are cheaper to insure than large higher-powered ones.

■ Keeping the car in a garage at night if you live in a high crime area instead of leaving it in the street.

■ Passing your 25th birthday. Premiums are much heavier for young drivers. An 18-year-old may pay twice as much as a 25-year-old.

■ Giving up using the car for business so that it can be insured for 'social, domestic and pleasure' use only which is cheaper.

■ Changing your job from one that carries 'loaded' premiums to one that is considered by the insurance companies to be less risky. Some companies load premiums for people such as publicans and journalists but not for, say, civil servants or bank workers.

■ Moving from a busy traffic-clogged city to a quiet neighbourhood.

Changes in Your Circumstances If you don't tell the insurance company of any changes in your circumstances they may not pay up if you make a claim. Apart from the disappointment you'll have wasted all the money you've spent on premiums.

Tell them if: Younger drivers are going to be using your car. Or if there is any change in the 'named' driver on your policy;

There's some change to your health that could affect your driving. If, for instance, you are diagnosed as diabetic or your eyesight fails. You should not only tell your insurance company but also the DVLC at Swansea. If you're not sure whether you have a condition you ought to report, ask your doctor's advice;

You've had an accident, summons or conviction since the last policy was issued;

Any modifications have been made to the car, especially if they affect its performance or value.

When the renewed policy has been issued check that any amendments have been made.

TIP *If you are selling your car and hand over keys, logbook and vehicle to a stranger who vanishes leaving you with a cheque or Banker's Draft that turns out to be forged don't expect the insurance company to pay up. It may be theft but you are in breach of your policy conditions which say you must take reasonable steps to prevent loss. You've not just left the keys in the car, which would be careless enough, but you've actually handed them over!*

Holiday Insurance

Everyone needs insurance when taking a holiday abroad. But you can easily be sold the wrong policy at the wrong price. Very often the company you are booking with will suggest you take out an inclusive package holiday.

Sometimes you never even get to see the policy and it isn't until you have to make a claim that you find out that it doesn't cover the particular circumstances of your claim.

Don't accept the reassurance of the travel agent or whoever is selling you the policy that it will cover all your likely needs. They may try to fob you off with a leaflet that merely summarises the main benefits. Or refer you to the summary of benefits in the tour operator's brochure.

At the risk of seeming difficult, insist on seeing the policy document. Even then you may have difficulty in understanding the gobbledegook in which some of these policies are written or even in reading the tiny print.

But stick with it. It's a waste of money if it doesn't provide the cover you want.

Basic cover The policy should cover you for:

- Cancellation or curtailment of your holiday because of

accident, illness, quarantine, pregnancy (that you didn't know about when you took out the policy), jury service or witness summons.

Parts of this should apply to close members of your family or business associates either travelling with you, or remaining at home. Some policies include cover for cancellation through strikes or adverse weather conditions, or redundancy as long as you've been employed for at least a year.

- Delay if your departure is held up beyond a specified period as a direct result of strikes, industrial action, adverse weather or mechanical breakdown of the aircraft or sea vessel.

TIP *Buy your insurance before or when you pay the deposit so that you're covered if you have to cancel before you depart.*

- Personal accident while on holiday resulting in death or permanent disablement, or loss of an eye or a limb. But you should have year-round cover for this if anyone would suffer as a result of you being killed or seriously injured.

- Personal liability for injury or damage caused to others or their property.

- Medical expenses including treatment, additional hotel or travelling expenses relating to the illness or returning home due to injury, illness or death of a friend or business associate travelling with you. Medical expenses under a package policy may not be sufficient for North America and you may have to take out additional insurance.

Don't rely on the reciprocal medical health service arrangements within the countries of the EC. They probably won't cover the full cost and you won't be covered for any additional travel and accommodation expenses.

- Your luggage and articles worn or carried should be covered against loss or damage. Losses must be reported to the police within 24 hours and you will need proof that you've done this.

But the insurance company probably won't pay out if you haven't taken care of valuables. They may not reimburse you, for instance, if you left your handbag on the beach while you went for a swim and it's stolen. Keep valuables on you or locked away in a safe.

Most policies allow up to £50 so you can buy some emergency essentials if your luggage is delayed.

Some tour operators offer incentives so you'll insure with them when you book your holiday. Only consider these if the policy gives you the cover you want.

You'll need a special policy to cover you for injuries or death if you're going to be taking part in dangerous sports such as parachuting or rock climbing.

Take the policy with you on holiday (and the brochure) in case you run into problems. Get all the evidence you can on the spot to back up any claim you might make later.

Life Insurance

If you have dependants who would need money if you died, consider taking out life insurance. It's also a way of saving.

Unfortunately it's often sold by fast-talking sales reps who are so eager to get you to sign up – so that they can get their commission – that they don't give you the full facts and you can end up buying the wrong policy.

There are two main types of life insurance:

■ Protection only, known as 'term insurance', pays out if you die within a set number of years. It's relatively cheap and can be a good buy for someone with a young family and not much cash to spare. You can choose a policy that pays out a lump sum to your dependants or one that pays them a regular tax-free income. You decide how long you want the policy to run – perhaps while the children are at school. You don't get anything back if you survive until the end of the agreed term.

■ Investment-type insurance is a way of making long-term savings for the future that gives you some life cover in case you die. It pays out at the end of the agreed term or if you die beforehand.

TIP *Before you take out a policy, check to see if your firm's pension scheme already provides you with life cover. It may be enough.*

The main kinds of investment-type insurance are:

■ A with-profits endowment policy that guarantees the amount you will get when the policy matures but you also get bonuses which depend on the success of the company's investments. It also pays out if you die.

■ Low cost endowment policy, that is used mainly to repay mortgage loans. Bonuses are added so that by the time the policy matures there should be enough to pay off the mortgage and something over. The mortgage is paid off if you die.

■ Unit-linked policies buy units in investment funds. What you get when you cash them in depends on the value of the units at the time. You get some life cover.

■ Whole life policies pay out an agreed sum on your death, whenever it is. It's a way of saving up for your dependants. It's not such a good deal for young people under 35 because it ties up money for a long time. But it can be useful for older people in case future health problems make it hard to get insurance.

TIP *If you cash in a life policy early you probably won't even get back the money you've paid in. If you need cash urgently you should be able to get a low-interest loan against the surrender value of the policy. If you can't afford the premiums try to get the policy 'paid up'. You then pay no more premiums but your family will still have some cover, although not as much as if you had continued paying.*

Think twice before accepting advice to surrender an existing policy with one insurance company and take out a policy with another. You'll almost certainly lose money on your first policy.

If you are thinking of taking out a life policy or a salesman calls on you ask yourself these questions:

■ Do I need it? If no one will suffer financial loss if you died – if, for instance, you are single and without dependants – you don't need this kind of insurance. You would do better with another form of saving which doesn't include life cover – for which you pay through your premiums.

■ Have I already got sufficient life cover either through my employer or some other savings plan? Of course, if you change your job you may lose the benefit of life cover and have to consider taking out separate insurance.

■ How much protection do I want to buy? It will depend on such circumstances as whether your partner works or is likely to, how many children you have and how old they are.

Work out what your dependants would get if you died today and what they would need. Allow for outgoings saved (the mortgage, for instance, would probably be paid off) and income lost (your take-home pay, pension etc).

The difference between the two is the amount of insurance you would need now plus an allowance for future needs and inflation.

■ Which type of insurance should I take out? If it's mainly security for your family you need, protection-only insurance gives much more cover for your money than investment-type insurance.

If you want investment-type insurance keep in mind that you must keep paying over a long period or you'll lose out.

■ Where should I get it? Not from the first insurance salesman who knocks at your door. Get quotes from several companies. Company reps sell only their company's product. An independent financial adviser can offer advice on a wider range of policies but may be limited to investment-only types.

If you're not convinced that the policy that is being sold to you is the right one, don't commit yourself. If you do decide to buy, be certain you know what you're buying.

You'll be given a 14-day cooling-off period in which you can cancel the deal (unless you bought a single premium type policy by sending off a form). If you change your mind after the 14 days you could lose some or all of any money you have already paid.

ELEVEN

Banks and Building Societies

Many people have no idea whether their money is in the best bank or building society account. That's hardly surprising given the number of accounts that are available and their advantages and disadvantages. Even the experts find it difficult to pick their way through the fine print of each deal.

All banks offer basic services such as: paying in facilities, cheque-books, cheque guarantee cards, automatic cash machines so you can draw money from your account or check your balance at any time of the day or night, credit cards, debit cards, standing orders, direct debits, overdrafts, personal loans, travellers' cheques and home banking.

You can have your salary paid into your account each month and arrange a separate account for large household bills. You can also take out insurance or a pension, use the bank's investment service or keep valuable documents or articles in their safe.

Most of the big building societies offer some or all of the basic facilities but not all the services.

Initially, their big attraction as an alternative to using the bank was that they paid interest on current accounts. Banks have reacted to this competition by launching new accounts that also pay interest but they are less simple. And not all current accounts pay interest when you are in credit.

What You Need

■ An account into which your salary can be paid, which offers a cheque-book, the usual cards, and a full service;

■ An account that pays interest on your money when you're in credit;

■ A bank or building society branch that is close to home or to your workplace.

You may be able to fulfil all these needs with one bank or building society account. Or you may have to have two: perhaps a bank current account so you have access to the extra services that banks provide plus a building society account that pays interest when you're in credit and doesn't slap on charges when you slip into the red.

Keeping Tabs

Bank charges can be a nasty shock. Even if you're overdrawn by a few £s for a few days you can be charged for every cheque, standing order, direct debit and cash machine withdrawal during the 'charging period', which can be one or three months, plus a maintenance charge.

You'll also pay interest on the amount by which you are overdrawn and might be charged for bounced cheques or warning letters the bank manager has sent.

It's vital therefore to keep your account in the black unless you have an arrangement with your bank manager to overdraw. You have to pay for such an arrangement but charges are not as high as when you are overdrawn without an arrangement.

Don't leave too much money in a current account that doesn't pay interest. You have to strike a fine balance between ensuring that there's enough to keep you in credit but not so much that you're lending the bank spare cash interest-free.

You can use your cashcard to check your balance between statements. If you receive statements say only every three months ask the bank to send them once a month.

If you do accidentally slip into the red by a small amount for a few days write to your bank manager as soon as possible explaining why it has happened and ask if he could overlook the error on this occasion. Bank managers have discretionary powers and can arrange a refund of the interest and charges if they feel it was an uncharacteristic mistake on your part. But they won't make a habit of letting you off.

TIP Even without being overdrawn you can be landed with hefty charges for some of the banks' special services which have been increased to help off-set the cost of the new interest-paying current accounts. It can come as quite a shock to find you've been charged up to £5 a sheet for a duplicate statement or for stopping a cheque.

Paying gas, electricity or credit card bills over the counter can cost £2 at some banks, while getting a Banker's Draft to pay for a major item like a car can cost anything from £5 to £10.

If you want to cash a cheque at another branch and haven't got your cheque guarantee card with you it could cost £2-£3 plus the cost of the phone call.

So think twice before using your bank's special services. With some you won't find out just how much they've cost you until you get your next statement.

If there's any chance you might on occasions become overdrawn, you might think about switching to an account that charges you a fixed fee and allows you to be overdrawn up to an agreed limit without paying charges. But that's an extra payment you'll be making every month just to avoid bank charges. It could cost up to £120 a year.

Other new-style accounts charge you only if you overdraw or if you are overdrawn by more than £100, or after a certain number of days.

You would be better off with one of the building society accounts that doesn't charge you for being overdrawn and that pays a good rate of interest on your credit balance.

TIP If it's getting towards the end of the month and you are worried that your current account is getting low, use your credit card instead of writing a cheque. Even if you can't pay off all that you owe on the card at the end of the month, the interest you pay won't hit you as hard as bank charges.

Bill Paying

Try to spread the payments of regular bills so that they don't all arrive at the same time. Ask the gas, electricity and water authorities if you could alter payment dates.

Another way to ease the bill burden is to stagger payments through the year by paying so much a month into a budget account. This is a good idea for the community charge and for water rates where the alternative is to dig into your funds and pay a lump sum in advance. By paying so much over the year you keep some of the money in your account earning interest.

You can also pay gas and electricity bills through a budget account. This gives you peace of mind but you can be paying in advance and may even be paying too much.

With mortgage payments that can fluctuate with changing interest rates it may be simpler to pay by direct debit. This should be a top priority bill and paying by direct debit ensures that it gets paid. Your TV licence could be paid the same way.

If there's any chance of you forgetting to pay your credit card bills, a direct debit arrangement will ensure that you don't run up interest charges. Pay from an interest-paying account.

Bank budget schemes also take the worry out of bill paying. With these you estimate what all your bills are likely to come to over a year, divide the total by 12 and pay this amount into the account each month. You then pay all your bills from the one account. But while some pay interest while you're in credit, you usually have to pay for the service. Pay bills by credit card to take advantage of the interest-free period.

The Mortgage

For most people there's a choice of two main types of mortgage: repayment and endowment.

With a repayment mortgage you pay back the money you borrow, usually monthly, together with interest over the length of the loan which is often 25 years. In the early years you are mostly paying back interest.

An endowment mortgage is linked to an insurance policy. You pay only interest on the loan and premiums on an insurance policy. When it matures the policy pays off the loan and may also give you a lump sum. There's no guarantee how much this will be. There are different kinds of endowment mortgage – the low-cost type is generally considered better than the others. One of the drawbacks of an endowment mortgage is that when interest rates increase it's not normally possible to ease the burden by extending the length of the loan.

■ When interest rates are increasing a fixed-rate mortgage may seem attractive, especially to a family on a limited budget. With this kind of loan, you pay a fixed rate for a certain period, normally two or three years, when you take out the loan, and after that pay the going interest rate.

It can give a sense of security while interest rates are rising. No matter how high they rise, you pay the same amount each month. But you will also be paying that same amount when interest rates fall and could be paying over the odds until the end of the period.

This kind of mortgage can be expensive if you try to switch to another lender or to a variable interest rate mortgage before the end of the fixed term.

■ Low-start mortgages also have their attractions, especially for young couples with not much money now but good prospects. You pay lower than normal interest in the early years and more later on.

Again there is a real possibility that you will find yourself paying a far higher interest rate than your neighbours in the future. You may also have to take out extra life insurance cover because of the extra debt.

■ Shared ownership schemes offer a chance to young couples who can't afford to get on to the home ownership ladder in the traditional way. You start by paying only part of the mortgage and the rest in rent. You pay a bigger proportion of the mortgage and pay less in rent when you can afford it.

See if your local authority runs such a scheme. Or contact the Housing Corporation, 149 Tottenham Court Road, London W1P 0BN.

TIP *Lenders may offer discounts to first-time buyers or borrowers wanting a larger loan. They are usually for a limited period. That's fine if everything else about the mortgage suits you, but don't be swayed by such inducements until you've checked that you can't get your mortgage cheaper elsewhere.*

Before you start to look for a mortgage do your sums. See how much you can afford to pay out each month on the mortgage and keep in mind that interest rates can rise taking a bigger slice out of your income each month. Will you still be able to pay the mortgage if one of you stops work or is ill or you split up?

Until recently, with house prices rising, being a home-owner seemed a manageable way of acquiring a valuable capital asset. Many people took on the biggest mortgage they could manage. But the fall in house prices and the rise in interest rates resulted in thousands losing their homes because they couldn't keep up with ever-rising repayments.

To avoid getting caught in the mortgage trap:

■ Work out a budget so you know what you can afford;

■ Don't borrow up to your limit. Rising interest rates may mean you can no longer afford the repayments and you may lose your home.

■ Shop around for the best loan deal. Compare the APR (Annual Percentage Rate of charge) interest figures. You may see other figures quoted but this is the one you should use in order to make comparisons. It won't include the cost of an endowment policy if you choose an endowment mortgage.

■ Read the small print of the agreement. Are there penalties for paying off early or will you have to pay a fee for arranging your own buildings insurance?

■ Find out exactly what your monthly costs will be. Check whether you will have to pay a penalty if you want to swap to a different type of mortgage or another lender later on. See what insurance cover you will need.

Cost is an important factor but getting the type of mortgage that suits your needs and that is backed up by good service is just as important.

Re-Mortgaging

When the going gets tough and you can't keep up mortgage repayments you may decide to look around to see if you can get a cheaper mortgage elsewhere.

Check the small print of your agreement before you do anything. You may have to pay a heavy penalty which will wipe out any gain you make.

Some lenders make no charge for ending a mortgage early, others charge several months interest or a fixed early redemption fee. Some lenders only charge if a mortgage is paid off in the early years. Switching to a cheaper loan can easily cost you several hundred £s.

With a fixed interest mortgage, where you have agreed to pay a set rate for a set time, you are likely to pay heavily if you try to get out of the arrangement when interest rates drop.

Some lenders that offer second mortgages so you can pay off the first and have money for other things such as home improvements can be much tougher than high street building societies if you can't keep up repayments.

Problems

Your home is the most important thing you possess so if you are having difficulty paying the mortgage contact the lender as soon as possible. It could mean the difference between having your home repossessed and finding a way around the problem.

The worst thing you can do is to sit on the problem and hope that it will go away.

Depending on your circumstances and the type of mortgage you have, the lender may be able to help by:

■ Switching you into a different type of mortgage that reduces your repayments;

■ Extending the period of the loan;

■ Offering a repayment 'holiday' while you try to get your affairs sorted out – a possibility for someone going through a temporary crisis such as being made redundant but with prospects of getting another job.

■ Letting you pay interest only for a limited time.

Most large building societies offer an annual scheme with monthly payments adjusted only once a year, regardless of how often during the year interest rates change.

An offer to make reduced payments until your problems have eased – or interest rates have fallen – might well be accepted by the building society or bank. But the offer must be realistic because if you can't keep up these payments you could lose your home. But lenders don't want to lose customers or to repossess homes if it can be avoided.

Some building societies have Helplines which offer debt counselling. Others have different, but similar, arrangements.

If you're in deep trouble visit your local Citizens' Advice Bureau. They'll probably have someone who is an expert at money problems and who may be able to negotiate with the building society and other creditors to try to sort things out.

You may have to rearrange your commitments and put off paying the less vital debts while you sort out the important ones such as the mortgage.

You'll have to make sacrifices too – perhaps return all your credit cards, give up holidays, send back the rented video/TV, and cut spending to the bone.

You may be entitled to claim social security benefits. Ask at your local Department of Social Security.

Protection Policy

If you have an endowment-type mortgage you get life insurance cover with it. But you don't get this protection with a repayment mortgage.

You can, however, take out a relatively cheap mortgage-protection policy that would pay off all you owe should you die. But policies taken out a few years ago may not have kept pace with later higher rates of inflation. The insurance company is unlikely to alert you to this so you should consider reviewing your policy if interest rates continue to be high.

You can also take out insurance which will pay off your mortgage if you are made redundant or become ill. The more you borrow the more important it is to have insurance cover.

TWELVE

Borrowing

Most people need to borrow money at some time or other, whether it is to buy a house, a car, a domestic appliance or to pay for a holiday.

Used wisely, credit can work to your advantage. You can buy expensive things such as a home or a car that would otherwise be out of reach. If your cooker blows up and you have to buy another immediately credit can help to spread the cost. It can also help spread the cost of expensive times such as Christmas.

You can borrow money by using your credit card and not to pay any interest because you pay off what you owe at the end of each month. If you time your purchases and payments carefully, you can get up to 56 days interest-free credit.

Or you can take advantage of interest-free loans which shops sometimes offer as an inducement to get you to buy their products. You must watch out, though, that whatever you're buying isn't dearer than if you bought elsewhere.

But credit can be a dangerous temptation to spend beyond your means. Many people with serious debt problems started off by using their cards to buy what they liked when they liked, vaguely expecting that they'd be able to pay off their credit card account when it came in.

When they couldn't, they'd pay off the minimum and hope they could pay off the rest next time. But you have to pay interest on money owed and so the debt starts to roll up.

Store cards are an extra temptation. Don't forget that the only reason they're issued is that the store hopes you'll spend more money with them.

Credit cards may be the most popular way of borrowing money but they are not the only way. There are other ways of raising cash, some of which are cheaper.

Before you take that first step consider:

■ Do you really want to buy this item or is it just a passing fancy?

■ How urgently do you need it? Unless it's a bargain you know you'll never get again, could you save up the cash for it and buy in a week or a month or so?

■ Will you be able to afford to pay back what you owe? Study your budget and see how much you have to spare after all normal expenses have been paid. Don't run it too tight. You may have to dip into savings for an emergency.

■ Could you get the money from somewhere else – a savings account or a relative, perhaps? Even if you draw money from savings you'll probably be better off than with a loan.

■ Will you be able to pay your way when you are losing a chunk out of your weekly or monthly income in repayments? Remember that the loan is probably going to run for some time.

■ Interest rates can rise. If it's a variable loan the interest rates may go down – or up. Could you cope if your repayments increased?

■ If your income drops for any reason – illness, redundancy, a two-income family becoming a one-income family, for instance, – could you keep up the repayments? You can take out insurance to cover your repayments against this kind of event but it's expensive.

■ If you can't pay and get into trouble with the loan company you could find it difficult to borrow money in the future. You may not be able to get a mortgage for a house.

Shopping For Credit

If you do need to borrow to buy something don't accept the first deal that is offered. If you're buying a video, for instance, the shop may offer to arrange the credit deal for you. But you may be able to borrow the money more cheaply elsewhere.

It's as important to shop around for credit as it is to shop around for anything else you buy.

If the shop is offering interest-free credit that might be a bargain. But check that what you're buying can't be bought cheaper elsewhere and make sure that the repayments don't add up to more than the cash price. Sometimes there are hidden charges.

The simplest way to find the best credit deal is to compare the APR (Annual Percentage Rate of charge). This has to be worked out in a uniform way so that customers can compare like with like. As a general guide, the lower the APR figure the less you'll have to pay.

TIP *Always ask for a written quotation that you can take home and study. (They must give you one if you ask for it.) It makes it easier to compare different deals.*

If the interest rate is variable the interest charges can go up or down. But if it's a fixed interest loan you pay the same amount each month. This might make it easier to budget when money's tight.

If you need a big loan, perhaps for a car, and you haven't time to shop around a credit broker can help you find one.

TIP *If you don't take up a loan within six months the broker can charge you no more than £3 – as long as the loan was to be for £15,000 or less, or was for buying a house.*

Read the loan papers carefully before you sign. If there's anything you don't understand ask whoever is arranging the deal to explain it. Take extra care if a member of the sales staff has filled in the details for you. Make sure they are correct.

TIP *Some credit schemes provide insurance which will ensure that repayments continue if, for any reason, you can't continue paying. Often this insurance is included automatically unless you tick a box saying you don't want it. You may not want to pay the additional cost so look out for the box or ask if insurance is included and say if you don't want it. Even if you do you may be able to get it cheaper elsewhere. Some of these policies don't cover the self-employed or part-time workers or certain age groups such as pensioners. If you fall into any of these*

122

categories you would be wasting money to have an insurance-included deal.

With some loans settling-up very early on can prove expensive. At best you'll probably have to pay some of the interest you would have paid if the loan had run for the full period.

Credit Cards

The most popular way of borrowing. They are accepted in a wide variety of outlets and can be used for withdrawing money from cash machines.

You are given an individual credit limit and can spend up to that limit in any one month. You can either pay off all that you owe each month or pay a minimum amount, which is usually either £5 or 5% of what you owe, whichever is the larger. If you don't pay off all you owe you will be charged interest.

TIP *If you pay for anything costing more than £100 by credit card and you run into problems with the retailer, you can claim from the credit card company. They have 'joint liability' if anything goes wrong. If, for instance, you buy a faulty video from a shop which then goes bust, you can claim from the card company. Or if you'd booked a holiday and the tour company went bust you could claim compensation from the card company.*

The main drawback to credit cards is that it's tempting to let the amount you owe grow each month. It can become progressively more difficult to pay it off.

On the plus side, they save you carrying around a chequebook and a lot of money, and it's useful to be able to quote your credit card number when you want to order something by phone. They can be used at overseas banks to make cash withdrawals.

Bank credit cards belong to one of two international organisations, Visa or Mastercard/Access – and sometimes both. Some building societies also issue credit cards.

The days when they were issued free could be on the way out. Lloyds was the first of the big banks to charge a £12 per year fee on its Mastercard (in exchange for lower interest rates) and other banks could follow suit. If you don't usually pay off what you owe each month it may pay you to pay a fee and lower interest rates.

But if you don't use the card much or always pay off what you owe then it would pay to switch to a no-fee card.

If you are thinking of changing cards, shop around. Charges can vary considerably.

You may decide to cut up all your cards if plans, now in hand, go ahead for credit card holders to be charged more for goods and services than people paying by cash. The Government has approved the idea and has started discussions on how it might work.

TIP *Take advantage of perks offered by credit card companies. Most provide travel accident insurance (but check whether it is enough for your needs), for holidays or air fares when you pay the deposit with their credit card. Other perks include: discounts on holidays and certain goods, bonus points which can be collected and exchanged for goods, charity donations, and discounts on car insurance, car hire and tyres.*

Store Cards

Many high street stores and retail chains offer customers their own credit card. They are similar to bank credit cards: if you pay off what you owe each month no interest is charged or you can have extended credit and pay interest on the outstanding balance.

Others have a budget account where you pay in so much every month and can borrow up to 20 or 30 times that amount. Interest is charged on the outstanding balance. These accounts can be useful if you know you are going to do a lot of shopping in one store, or as a way of spreading the cost of Christmas. But if you're not, the amount you pay in each month will build up and *you* won't get interest on it.

Interest rates on these cards are generally higher than for many other forms of borrowing. But there are add-on benefits such as invitations to previews for the sales, discounts not available to other customers and maybe free catalogues.

TIP *If you are thinking of taking out a store card ask if they have any special promotions coming up where you get a discount for joining.*

Charge And Gold Cards

American Express and Diners are the two best known. You pay a fee to join and an annual fee. Unlike credit cards, you don't get credit and there is no spending limit. You must pay off what you owe each month. You may be able to get big unsecured overdrafts.

Hire Purchase

You pay a deposit on something you want to buy – perhaps a car or a video – and make weekly or monthly repayments. The agreement must show the cash price, the total hire purchase price and the amount of each repayment.

You don't own the goods until the last payment has been made. So you can't sell them while still making the repayments. And if you don't keep up payments the HP company can take them back, although if you've paid a third of the money owed they would need a court order.

You don't have to take up the HP that's offered by the shop or garage. You might get a loan cheaper elsewhere. A bank personal loan, for instance, might cost you less.

Credit sale works in a similar way except that the goods belong to you once the deposit is paid.

Check Trading

You buy checks of differing values which can be used to pay for goods in certain shops instead of cash. You repay the check trader in weekly instalments, with interest.

This is available only in some parts of the country. It may be convenient but it's an expensive form of credit.

Bank Or Building Society Loans

If you have a bank account and need a loan to cover a big purchase, a bank ordinary loan could be cheapest. But not all banks offer them and those that do can be choosy about who gets one.

A personal loan generally costs a little more but is more readily available and is quick and simple to arrange. You can apply to your bank or you may be able to get one from a building society. You can ask for a lump sum which you pay back in regular instalments over an agreed period. The rate of interest is fixed from the start so that you know exactly what you are going to be paying back each month. You may have to pay a penalty if you pay off early.

If you are facing a temporary emergency or you think your account may slip into the red in the coming months you can ask your bank or building society for an overdraft facility. You can have one for a limited time or arrange for it to run for a longer period. It enables you to write cheques for more money than is in your account. You pay interest on the amount that is overdrawn, not on the full overdraft limit.

On top of interest you may also have to pay bank charges. But it is cheaper than letting your account slip into the red without getting the bank or building society manager's permission first.

TIP *Beware of secured loans. They may sound comforting and be cheaper than other loans but the money you borrow is secured on your home. That means that if, for any reason, you can't keep up the repayments you could lose your most valuable possession – the roof over your head!*

Save And Borrow Accounts

You pay in a set amount each month and can borrow up to say 30 times the monthly payment. You have a cheque-book and can use the money you pay in to pay regular bills. You may be paid a small amount of interest when the account is in the black but you pay interest when it falls into the red.

Finance Company Loans

Shops, car dealers and gas or electricity boards may offer to arrange a finance company loan if you're buying an expensive item. You may be able to get the money for less elsewhere so shop around before signing up. You could probably get a cheaper loan from the bank.

Credit Unions

These are co-ops where a group of people get together to save and to lend to each other. They may be members of the same street, club or church, or people who work together. Members pay a small joining fee and then save a regular amount. They elect a committee to run their affairs.

They receive a low rate of interest on their savings but can also borrow at extremely low rates – a maximum of 12.68%, which is the legal limit. Unions can lend up to £5,000 to a member plus another £5,000 if he has £5,000 savings in the unions.

They are an excellent way of saving and borrowing small sums of money. Repayments are arranged to suit the borrower. If you are interested in setting up a DIY loan scheme with friends contact: The Association of British Credit Unions, Ltd., 48 Maddox Street, London W1R 9BB or the National Federation of Credit Unions, 1-3 Fairfax Crescent, Bierley, Bradford BD4 6BP.

TIP *If you repay a loan early you might not save as much as you think. Lenders are entitled to charge a penalty to cover their costs in setting up the loan.*

Problems

If you can't keep up your loan repayments tell the lender as soon as possible. Don't just stop making payments.

Offer to pay off what you owe in instalments that you know you can keep up. It may tie up all your money for a long time but it's better than having a county court judgement made against you. Once this happens it will affect your creditworthiness and you will find it very difficult to borrow money in the future.

If you can't see a way out of your difficulties get help from the money adviser at your Local Citizens' Advice Bureau or Trading Standards/Consumer Protection Department which is run by the local authority. You'll find the address in the Phone Book.